GET
FRESH BOOKS

Praise for POET OF ONE ISLAND

With the raw honesty of a poet digging up the earth of his colonized homeland, Jacques Viau Renaud's calls for racial justice in these translations echo with shards of Whitmanesque rhapsody cutting across the Americas.

-**Roger Sedarat,** translator of Forthcoming: *This Garden Night: Ghazals of Hafez*

Viau's verse is a gift of irony that aches between the beauty of this island and reveals true agony haunting his homeland. Viau writes with heart amid anger for a people divided by power of privilege, whose oppression and wealth slices this geography of pain, but not the metaphors of this brave poetic spirit, Viau taken too soon, whose wisdom still fans like "lilies blooming," as in the origin story of "Quisqueya," the one-island homeland before sliced by colonial forces, "this island trapped in a tear." In Viau's PraiseSong/Elegy to Medgar Evers, he captures the hateful racism of Jim Crow America, where Evers fights injustice. A PraiseSong/Elegy hails Walt Whitman's power and legacy still speaking, no more profoundly in Viau's "Song for America," his litany of critique calling America to "shake off the dust and rust inside . . . ," its insidious support of the Caribbean. In Viau's home, in the poem "The Rain," whether sex workers, their guards, or those who hustle them, "rebellion / is pulled from the people like roots / that clean the grim past / lifting up life." Viau is intense, instructive, and radical, captures disappointment that injustice rains on people, teaches a deep understanding of that complex, but leaves us hopeful, since like his love of homeland in singing amid suffering, "rebellion lifts life," his verse—his voice, a refuge, his hand "a bridge / between … cries."

-**Dr. Mona Lisa Saloy,** author of *Black Creole Chronicles*

Also by Ariel Francisco:

Poetry:
All the Places We Love Have Been Left In Ruins (2024)
Under Capitalism if Your Head Aches They Just Yank Off Your Head (2022)
Every Day Now I Wake Up With a Mouth Full of Blood (2021)
A Sinking Ship is Still a Ship (2020)
All My Heroes Are Broke (2017)
Before Snowfall, After Rain (2016)

Translations:
Moonless Night by Francisco Henriquez (2024)
Hard Equilibrium by Mateo Morrison (2024)
Burning of Reichstag by Cristian Gomez Olivares (2024)
*Selections From "Permanence of the Cry" and Other Poems
by Jacques Viau Renaud* (2024)
Routines/Goodbyes by Hael Lopez (2022)
Voyage by Carolina Sanchez (2020)

Get Fresh Publishing, A Non-Profit Corp.
PO Box 901
Union, NJ 07083

www.gfbpublishing.org

ISBN: 9798218360023

Library of Congress Control Number: 2024935566
Cover, layout, typesetting, and design:
Anny Caba | AnnyCaba.com

Photographs on the cover used with the permission of Michelle Viau. Photos by Viau Renaud, Jacques. Permanencia del llanto. Santo Domingo, Frente Cultural, 1965.

This book was typeset in Arkhip, Helvetica, and Times New Roman

Contents

POET OF ONE ISLAND

Selected Poems of
Jacques Viau Renaud

Translated by
Ariel Francisco

POET OF ONE ISLAND:
ON THE REVOLUTIONARY POETICS OF JACQUES VIAU RENAUD

In the turmoil and chaos after the long awaited death of the dictator known as El Jefe, Rafael Trujillo, in 1961 between the ousting of democratically elected president Juan Bosch in 1963 and the subsequent April Revolution of 1965, the poetry of Jacques Viau Renaud entered the divided land of the Dominican Republic as both a call to arms and a cry for unity. His dual identity as Haitian-Dominican and the duality of his revolutionary ideals both as poet and as rebel survive as a testament to his commitment and love for his adopted homeland and to the urgency and timelessness of his poetry. Viau was born in Port-au-Prince in 1941, just four years after the horrors of the Parsley Massacre. He followed his father, a school teacher, into political exile in the Dominican Republic in 1948. Perhaps it was this forced familiarity with displacement so early in life that led to his early death, dying in 1965 at the age of twenty-three, laying down his life for Dominican independence and democracy against the authoritarian coup backed up by an invasion of 40,000 US soldiers.

According to poet and scholar Mateo Morrison, "the time period of September 25th 1963 to April 24th 1965 was one of the most intense and distraught in our country's history" [the dates of the coup to oust President Bosch and the start of the revolution, respectively] and yet it is precisely during this tumultuous time that a young Viau began to develop his poetic voice and furiously write the poems he left behind. From the beginning, the notion of revolution permeated his writing. In "From the Mountains," dated June 5, 1963, Viau writes of the 1959 failed invasion of the towns of Constanza, Maimón, and Estero Hondo by rebels to overthrow Trujillo:

Constanza, Maimón, Estero Hondo:
cracking from the light,
destroyed path,
crucified night,
June 14th 1959
march of unchained men
stopped in the blood.
June 14th 1963
from the blood
men march anew
towards the unchained.

His support of the rebels and their ideals is clear in his metaphors and imagery, describing their defeat with the brief yet powerful depiction of "crucified night," capturing the immense proportions of their martyrdom in his eyes. His admiration for them comes through as well when he describes their actions as the "march of unchained men." Already, we see the seeds of a revolutionary fighter in the words of a revolutionary writer. If these men, in open rebellion to Trujillo's dictatorship, who willingly died for their anti-imperialist beliefs, are unchained, than what does that make him? He is chained and knows this, though he aspires (and will later become) one of the men who "march anew / towards the unchained." Viau pays homage to the 14th of June Revolutionary Movement (as it came to be known) as a predecessor and direct inspiration to the revolutionary sentiment and movement that was ramping up at the time, and that would ultimately lead to the April Revolution of 1965 while also setting himself down that same path. He operates as prophet for both the Dominican Republic and for himself: he is one of the men born "from the blood" of those rebels, and already he knows it is a cause worth dying for if it inspires others to continue that march; he is evidence of that inspiration and knows his forthcoming death will be the same.

Viau turns his lens to the United States as well, most poignantly in "For an Assassinated Black Leader," his powerful elegy for Medgar Evers and the subsequent marches, written within months of his murder. The poem opens with the lines "All the white shadows were conjured / to kill a black man." Immediately and concisely, Viau lays bare the racist foundations and structures of the United States by focusing our attention not on the assassin who actually pulled the trigger, but rather on the power structures of hatred that enable and encourage this kind of violence. He is implicating all of white America in Evers's death, and continues to invoke the word "white" to depict its violence. Describing the marches launched in response to the assassination, he deliberately places the explicit and direct "white hate" between two metaphors in this excerpt:

They murdered a black man.
Fury paved the landscape
the South crunched under the black march
that thundered from the cemetery

...

Medgar Evers
from the grave armed the black anger
slamming it over the white claw
over the white hate
over the white gallows
while in his dirt filled mouth
grow lilies.

Both "claw" and "gallows," when paired with "white", operate as jarringly effective metaphors for the deadly grip racism and white supremacy have in the United States and the desperate need to break out of that grip. Again, with the "white claw" and "white gallows," Viau reminds us that it was not just the man who pulled the trigger who killed Evers but a white society creating and enabling the murder, a white society that would allow the murder of a black man to go unconvicted. Viau is tragically aware of the acute possibility of dying for what you believe in, not as some imagined grand sacrifice but as a reality of oppression. With the line "from the grave armed the black anger" and "while in his dirt filled mouth / grow lilies," Viau creates an image of the revolutionary man still working and contributing to the greater cause even after death, as with the rebels in "From the Mountains" and the men marching anew. He is a part of the "black anger" armed by Evers but one of the lilies as well. Here, Viau's revolutionary duality is most resonant: yes, violence begets violence, but love begets love as well, the love for a people and a movement, the love to continue fighting. Again, we see Viau seeing a glimpse into his bloody future and not turning away. The poem's end, "Oh America, / concrete / heaps of the unlynched", speaks to the Dominican Republic as well as the US: countries built on the backs of slaves, black suffering, and black death.

The notions and complexities of what constitutes his "homeland" are other major themes in Viau's work. The word *Patria* appears thirty-five times in these attempts in his poems to reunite his birth home of Haiti with his adopted home of the Dominican Republic. His poems strain to reconcile these two countries that share an island, to stitch them back together. In "My Homeland Arose" he writes:

Like this my homeland emerged from this mourning life
with frayed pages and uncertain steps
like the dead bursting from their tombs,
distributing lots of silence to the landless peasants
sweating in anguish.

In both metaphor and image, he depicts the anguish, violence, and death that birthed both countries when he describes them as having emerged from "this mourning life" and the harsh reality of the peasant's life. These conditions exist in both countries, and Viau is creating a mirror with his lines to show the kinship between their respective inhabitants, however brutal. He takes this further in the last few lines of "I'm Trying to Tell You About My Homeland":

I've been trying to tell you about my homeland,
of my homelands,
of my island
that has long divided man
there, where they came together to create a river.

Here, there is no mistaking his desire to reconcile his two countries and his ultimate inability to do so. The transition of the singular "homeland" to the plural "homelands" is a tragic amendment to this attempt at reconciliation: though it is a singular island, as the poem progresses, it is the speaker himself who is reconciled, realizing that he cannot make these two countries into one "homeland," but rather that he actually has two "homelands," two "patrias." The complexity of this realization is deepened by the ending image, which refers to the Dajabon River on the Haitian-Dominican border: on the one hand, it is a border, the scene of endless violence (also called the Massacre River), and the line that "has long divided man," as the poems says; but on the other hand, describing the two countries as coming together to "create a river" is an undoubtedly beautiful image of unity and harmony. This image presents the possibility of the river as a symbol of unification instead of division, something life-giving stitching together the island that's been split in two by a history of human violence. Viau attributes agency to the two countries when he says "they came together to create a river"; he is not speculating but rather recounting it as fact. The failure, then, to view this unification as a dividing line is on humankind.

Viau does make another, possibly successful, attempt at reunification, though. In his poem "The Dead" (featuring the word "patria" three times), which focuses on the post-Trujillo destruction and violence and lauds the guerrilla fighters, he uses personification to amplify the damage being done to his home. He describes:

They raised their voices to defend their homeland
because she was dying
from so much spilled blood
from her assassin sons.

They rose to the mountains
to save what was left of her,
the green skin of Quisqueyana life,
her belly wide with
virgin rocks and blind marble.

The "they" are the guerrillas, and the "she" is the island. While his use of "patria" is most consistent with the English "homeland," it can also more specifically mean "motherland" as well. Again, we have the division of a people as a primary theme: the sons defending their homeland and the "assassin sons," a broken family. But what's most exciting and unique about this poem is his use of "Quisqueyana." Quisqueya was thought to be the indigenous name (presumably Taino) of the island now made up of Haiti and the Dominican Republic, though this has since been disproven. This is not a frivolous or decorative use of the word. Viau is reaching as deeply as he can into language and history in order to convey his desire for peace in his homeland. He does not name the individual countries, because that would give credit to the division. He does not call it Hispaniola, which would invoke Columbus and Europe and the colonization that started centuries of violence and war. He reaches for the indiginous name that predates the division of the island to recall a time when it was whole, to remind himself, us as readers, and his fellow countrymen that the idea of peace and wholeness is not a myth or a dream, that it actually existed at one point. He invokes it as a place of origin, as a place that can be returned to (both literally and metaphoricaly). It's important to note that the word *Quisqueya* was thought to mean "mother of all lands" as well.

…

Jacques Viau Renaud, dead at age twenty-three— to me he is our Caribbean Keats: wise and talented beyond his years, taken from us too soon. We can only imagine the way his work could have continued to evolve had he lived. What he did write during his lifetime is incredibly important, especially to those who come from the diaspora caused by the revolution he fought in, and all revolutions fighting against fascism and imperialism. Viau's poetry should be read alongside that of his renowned countrymen Pedro Mir of the Dominican Republic and Jacques Roumain of Haiti; alongside his fellow fallen Latin American revolutionary poets like Otto René Castillo of Guatemala and Roque Dalton of El Salvador; alongside the Carribean Négritude poets like Aimé Césaire and René Depestre; along the Harlem Renaissance writers like Langston Hughes and Claude McKay. As both poet and revolutionary, Jacques Viau Renaud wrote poetry that is tragically as relevant today as it was when it was written, when he was killed. His poems are a call to arms, literally and figuratively, to oppressed peoples across the Americas, which resounds incredibly loudly with the state of the world today.

SURGÍA LA PATRIA

Surgía la patria de su enlutada vida
como una aislada brisa de yerba en los eriales.
El aire seco de las montañas
abrazaba nuestro rostro con su perfume de muertos
mientras el hambre caminaba los caminos del hombre.

La tierra se partía reseca.
Un cielo hostil se aferraba al sol
y a las nubes.
Nada caía de él.
Las hojas de los árboles se iban desprendiendo de su verdor
se iban desnudando
mientras los árboles agonizaban.
Los ríos se hacían lentos y perezosos
los pajarillos huían
del exhalado polvo de esta tierra
de aluminio y oro
de hambre larga y ancha sed.

Así la patria iba surgiendo de su enlutada vida
con deshilachados crespones y pasos torpes
como una muerta desde su tumba arrancada,
repartiendo lotes de silencio entre los campesinos sin tierras
húmedos de angustia.

La vida se iba repartiendo agonías
el hombre se levantaba como un cactus
en la soledad de los yermos
abriendo caminos entre la yerba escasa
y la piedra abundante.

El polvo ahogaba sus aullidos
y cubría sus llagas bajo el sol y el cielo
de esta tierra masacrada.

MY HOMELAND AROSE

My homeland arose from this mourning life
like a lone earthen breeze in the wastelands.
Dry air of the mountains
caresses our faces with the aroma of death
while hunger walks the path of man.

The dry earth split.
A hostile sky slings toward the sun
and the clouds.
Nothing falls.
The leaves on the trees abandon their green
going on naked
leaving the agonized trees to die.
The rivers become lethargic and tired
the birds flee
from dust exhaled by the earth
from aluminum and gold
from long hungers and widening thirst.

Like this my homeland emerged from this mourning life
with frayed pages and uncertain steps
like the dead bursting from their tombs,
distributing lots of silence to the landless peasants
sweating in anguish.

Life was doling out agony
man rose like a cactus
in the wasteland's solitude
opening paths in the scarce grass
and abundant rocks.

Dust drowned the howling
and smothered the sores under the sun and sky
of this massacred land.

ESTOY TRATANDO DE HABLAROS DE MI PATRIA

ESTOY tratando de hablaros de mi patria,
aquella que comienza a deslizarse
allá donde crecen las guazábaras,
las cayenas frágiles,
los cántaros sedientos y polvorientos,
la yerba rara,
amarillenta,
solitaria lanza midiendo el corazón de mi Isla.

ESTOY tratando de hablaros de mi patria,
desde aquí,
desde mi guarida salina,
desde Santo Domingo,
quizás os hable de ambas:
son dos terrones complementarios
puntos cardinales de mi tristeza
caídos de la rosa de los vientos
como amantes cuyo abrazo se rompieran.

ESTOY tratando de hablaros de mi patria,
de su prole de montes y altibajos,
de planicies soñolientas,
donde ha mucho parieron ríos:
muchedumbre de cristales apiñados en las hondonadas.

MI PATRIA
es una tierra elevada
de dilatados herbazales y doradas mazorcas
que cruzan los mares y se van muy lejos
mientras los hombres del monte y la llanura
se dilatan hambrientos.

Es una tierra con muchos montes pelados,
sonoros ríos de apaciguada fauna
y violentos vegetales...

I'M TRYING TO TELL YOU ABOUT MY HOMELAND

I'm trying to tell you about my homeland,
the one that begins to slip
where the guasabara trees grow,
the fragile peppers,
the thirsty dust-covered pitchers,
the strange
yellowish grass,
lonely spear measuring the heart of my island.

I'm trying to tell you about my homeland,
from here,
from my saline lair,
from Santo Domingo,
maybe I'll speak of both:
two sibling mounds
cardinal points of my sorrow
fallen from the wind's rose
like lovers breaking their embrace.

I'm trying to tell you about my homeland,
of her children, her peaks and valleys,
her sleepy plains
where countless rivers are born:
crowds of crystals huddled in the hollows.

My homeland
is a plateau
of betrayed green and golden maize
that cross the seas to go far off
while the people of the mountains and plains
grow with hunger.

It's a land of many bare mountains,
loud rivers of cheerful wildlife
and violent flora.

CRUJE mi patria al parir
y sus proles se reducen
y parecen hojas desprendidas
confundiéndose en los bosques con la magra corteza de los árboles.

ALLÍ, aprisionada entre dos brazos de arcilla,
roca y piedra,
duerme una ciudad que huele a muerto,
a caña madura,
a virgen alcohol terrosa
como resina de nudosas raíces destacadas.

ES UNA ciudad de calles sin nombres
y atajos de espanto,
habitada hasta en las grietas,
en las cloacas,
quedamente recorrida por las ratas y los murciélagos.

ES UNA ciudad de muchas proles numerosas,
de millares de niños que nunca crecieron,
que nunca supieron el color de los faroles
ni del alba con pan y sin lágrimas,
de niños que maduraron las tumbas,
la tierra apisonada adornada de girasoles,
y la luz de las pupilas ciegas.

ALLÍ he nacido,
de allí partí atado a la sangre,
solo, después de los años,
descubrí en mi pecho la mancha roja,
entonces aprendí a leer en las hojas,
a hablar con la tierra
y a callar cuando ella reconstruía la historia
de los muchos muertos que la sustentan,
de la sangre que alimentó sus frutas,
del llanto que sostuvo la precocidad de sus montes.

My homeland cracked giving birth
and her children wither
and look like dying leaves
confusing themselves in the forest of thin-barked trees.

There, imprisoned between two clay arms,
rock and stone,
sleeps a city that smells of death,
of sugarcane,
of earthly virgin liquor
like resin of great gnarled roots.

It's a city of nameless streets
and ghostly alleys
even the cracks hold life,
even the sewers,
quietly traversed by rats and bats.

It's a city full of countless children,
of countless children that never grow up,
that never learn the colors of lanterns
or dawn, with bread and without tears,
of children who ripen in tombs,
the tamped ground adorned with sunflowers,
and the light of blind eyes.

Here, I was born,
from here I left, tied to the blood,
alone, after years,
I found the red stain inside me,
and then learned to read the leaves,
to speak with the earth
and be quiet when she reconstructs the history
of the many dead that sustain her,
of the blood that fed her fruits,
the screams that sustained her precocious mountains.

MUCHO tiempo ha transcurrido desde que partí,
nada ha cambiado,
siguen los mismos montes pelados,
la misma vegetación de vegetales y girasoles,
de cafetales oscuros y pastizales estrellados,
sólo el hambre ha crecido,
ya no hay lugar en los cementerios
ni en los ojos llanto
ni en mi Isla patrias,
sólo dimensiones de tierra y harapo,
de muertos desencajados en el vientre del barro.

ASI es mi patria,
prolongación del Santo Domingo que llora,
así es mi guarida,
prolongación del grito que recorre los montes,
los caminitos,
los bosques,
desde el otro lado de la sangre,
desde la mole de San Nicolás,
hasta la frente de cristal salobre
y esqueletos de peces mudos amontonados sobre la playa
creciendo y haciéndose montañas
entre redes hambrientas y ahumados pescadores.
Allí los muertos se hacen peces hermosos,
algas extensas, musgo silencioso,
o acantilado de rumores que la noche protege.

HE QUERIDO hablaros de mi patria,
de mis dos patrias,
de mi Isla
que ha mucho dividieron los hombres
allí donde se aparearon para crear un río.

So much time has passed since I left,
nothing has changed,
those same bald mountains go on,
the same vegetation and sunflowers,
the same dark coffee fields and starry pastures,
only hunger has grown,
there's no more space in the cemeteries
or in the crying eyes
or in my island homeland,
only dimensions of dirt and rags,
of the dead unhinged from the mud by the wind.

This is my homeland,
an extension of Santo Domingo crying,
this is my haunt,
extension of the cry echoing from the mountains,
the roads,
the forests,
from the other side of the blood,
from the port of Saint Nicholas,
to the face of the brackish crystal
and the bones of deaf fish piled on the beach
becoming mountains
between hungry nets and sunburned fisherman.
Here the dead turn into handsome fish,
covered in algae, silent moss,
cliffs of rumors protected by the night.

I've been trying to tell you about my homeland,
of my homelands,
of my island
that has long divided man —
there, where they came together to create a river.

LA LLUVIA

La lluvia se abría sobre el pavimento
dibujando.
Ociosas prostitutas
semiescondidas
se guarecían
esperando algún tonto beodo
que vierta en sus enganchados encantos
su semanal hambre aguantada
de agrio sudor infecundo
de mujer que se rompe las uñas y los dedos
de niños que aguardan el plato siempre lejano
el postre extrañísimo.

La vida transcurría
los focos de los automóviles
asediaban las calles de impúdicas visiones.
La voracidad babeante de los callejones oscuros
abría orificios en la carne del hombre.

Los guardias
y sus fusiles
la policía y sus garrotes
el espía y su largo oído
anunciaban la sangre
anunciaban el estallido
anunciaban la muerte sobre las espaldas de la lluvia.
Finamente cayendo
como lianas transparentes y quebradizas
que dejan entre sí estrechas compuertas
por donde el aire se escapa seco
en esta noche de caluroso diciembre
abierto a la sangre
como una migaja abandonada en un puñado de hambre.

THE RAIN

Rain opens over pavement,
drawing.
Idle sex workers
half hidden
protecting themselves
waiting for some drunk idiot
to empty into their charmed hooks
holding in that weekly hunger
of sour sterile sweat
of women that break nails and fingers
of children awaiting a far-off plate
of strange dessert.

Life goes on
the car headlights
besiege the streets with lewd visions.
The drooling veracity of dark alleys
opens holes in the body of man.

The guards
and their rifles
the cops and their clubs
the spies and their long hatred
announcing the blood
announcing the outbreak
announcing the dead on the back of the rain.
Falling finely
like thin brittle vines
leaving narrow gates between them
where dry air escapes
in this hot December night
open to the blood
an abandoned crumb in a handful of hunger.

La vida transcurría.
Los guardias
y las prostitutas se hacían señas
y pronto las palabras no eran más que recuerdo.
Los niños
cubrían sus cuerpecitos con sus manos
pequeñitas
expuestos a la lujuria del tiempo.

Los grandes señores
codeando la noche cambiaban de ropaje
para extirpar de la infancia
la honradez todavía incipiente de los arrabales.

Los callejones aullaban un sucio espanto.
La noche se deshacía
se alejaban las estrellas
las prostitutas
cansadas
bostezando se marchaban,
mientras que un niño limpiabotas
empujaba las pocas puertas que del amor quedaban.

Diciembre con días sangrientos
y dilatados
empapados de savia rebelde
arrancada del pueblo como raíces
que van limpiando las mugrientas edades pasadas
levantando la vida.

Life goes on.
The guards
and sex workers signal each other
and soon words will only be memories.
The children
cover their small bodies with their hands
tiny
exposed to time's lust.

The large men
hustling through night change clothes,
remove their childhood
honor still incipient in the suburbs.

The alleys howl a dirty ghost.
Night comes undone
the stars back away
the women
tired
yawning, they march,
meanwhile a shoeshine kid
pushes the few doors left by love.

December of bloody
and dilated days
soaked with the sap of rebellion
pulled from the people like roots
that clean the grim past
lifting up life.

DESDE LAS MONTAÑAS

Desde las montañas dormidas en las faldas del viento
sube un rumor
de cenizas apretujadas.
Desde el follaje
la muerte sube
clavándose en el sol
y un grito desnudo vaga por las soledades
martillando el cerebro de un pueblo.

Constanza, Maimón, Estero Hondo:
tumbas creciendo hacia lo vegetal,
tumbas creciendo solas
hacia la sencillez del polvo
donde perecen las palabras
y los hombres.

Constanza, Maimón, Estero Hondo:
tumbas creciendo hacia el sol,
escalando la sangre,
asomándose a la piedra.
Constanza: desgarradura de la luz.
Maimón:
olas despedazando el verde calor de hombres
desnudos
iluminando la noche,
el día,
los meses y los años
iluminando.

FROM THE MOUNTAINS

From the mountains sleeping in the wind's skirts
rises a rumor
of pressed ash.
From the green
rise the dead
nailing themselves to the sun
a naked shout wanders through solitude
hammering the mind of a town.

Costanza, Maimón, Estero Hondo:
tombs growing toward the green,
tombs growing alone
toward the simplicity of dust
where words
and the human die.

Costanza, Maimón, Estero Hondo:
tombs growing toward the sun,
scaling the blood,
peering out of the stone.
Constanza: torn from the light.
Maimón:
waves shearing away the green heat
of naked men
illuminating the night,
the day,
the months and years
illuminated.

Estero Hondo:
grieta abierta en el viento,
en la senda del hombre en busca del hombre.
Constanza, Maimón, Estero Hondo,
arcilla, piedra y follaje
aprisionando la vida,
la vida asesinada desde las estrellas.

Cayeron
desde el luminoso aullido del costado herido
hablando con la yerba,
con los árboles
únicos protectores,
únicos amigos,
únicos en ser devorados por el mismo fuego;
en la misma senda
cayeron con el amanecer.

El viento de esta isla,
de esta isla aprisionada en una lágrima,
en una lágrima sola,
vegetal,
derrumbó la noche.

Se adentró en sus pechos la noche,
el fuego consumió sus miembros,
el odio y las cadenas
crucificaron la esperanza.
El viento recogió sus cenizas:
desde entonces
las guardas apretándolas a su seno,
a su rostro desdibujado
por la luz crucificada.

Estero Hondo:
an open shout in the wind,
on the path of man searching for man.
Costanza, Maimón, Estero Hondo,
clay, rock, and green
imprisoning life,
life assassinated by stars.

Fallen
from the luminous howl of the injured
speaking with the grass,
with the trees
only protectors,
only friends,
the only ones devoured by the same fire;
on the same path
fallen with the morning.

The wind of this island,
of this island trapped in a tear,
a single tear,
green,
collapsed in the night.

Night entered their stomachs,
fire consumed their limbs,
hatred and chains
crucifying hope.
The wind cleaned up the ashes:
since then
they're guarded tightly by the dream,
by the blurred face
by the crucified light.

Cayeron
pero su grito resuena,
martillea en la frente de un pueblo
que marcha hacia el día que nace.
Constanza, Maimón, Estero Hondo:
rajadura de la luz,
sendero dinamitado,
noche crucificada,
14 de junio 1959
marcha del hombre sin cadenas
detenida en la sangre.
14 de junio 1963
desde la sangre
marcha de nuevo el hombre
hacia el hombre sin cadenas.

Fallen
but the shout echoes,
hammering the town's face
marching toward the day of birth.
Costanza, Maimón, Estero Hondo:
cracking from the light,
destroyed path,
crucified night,
June 14, 1959
march of unchained men
stopped in the blood.
June 14, 1963
from the blood
men march anew
toward the unchained.

AMANECE EL HOMBRE

Amanece el hombre sembrando su simiente asesinada
cuajando la esperanza en un grito.
La luz se escapa de sus manos.
El arroyo de las lavanderas lanza su sonora risa
escurriéndose entre árboles
apretando la tierra
poseyéndola
dejando en sus raíces el semen puro de sus entrañas;
inyectándole toda su briosa mocedad
arrancándole todo su amor enterrado
todo el apretado silencio de los caminos de mi patria
asolada por el hambre
embestida por el robo
conducida en pedazos hacia los bancos
donde una jauría de disfrazados excrementos
acapara las azucenas y el pan.

Hombre de mi patria
caminante
andador
fatigada cerviz Antillana
aquí te tiendo mi mano para que sirva de puente
entre tu llanto y mi llanto
sobre ella deposita tu cabeza
deposita tu corazón en sus llagas
y escucha en silencio
cómo amanece
cómo chillan los pajarillos
cómo canta el arroyo de las lavanderas
disputándose
abriéndose como un surco
para que echemos en él nuestra sangre
y quizás
¿quién sabe? nuestra vida.

MAN AWAKENS

Man awakens sewing the assassinated seed
hope curdling in a cry.
Light escapes his hands.
The washer's stream throws its loud laughter
rinsing in the trees
tightening the earth
possessing it
leaving the internal seed in the roots;
injecting his spirited youth
unearthing the buried love
all the tightened silences in the streets of my homeland
razed by hunger
assaulted by thieves
led toward the banks in fragments
where pieces of shit in disguise
monopolize the lilies and bread.

Humanity of my homeland
wanderer
traveler
fatigued vertebrae of the Antilles
here I give my hand to serve as a bridge
between our cries
for you to rest your head
place your heart on the sores
and listen silently
how it dawns
how the birds squawk
how the river of lavender sings
fighting
opening a furrow
to pour our blood
and maybe,
who knows, our lives.

Hombre de todos los caminos.
del alba
enhiesta mole de esfuerzos derrumbados
estatua de mi patria
esculpida en la raíz profunda de la noche.
Toma mi mano
y escuchemos juntos
cómo amanece cantando el arroyo de las lavanderas
y los chillidos que se rompen pregonando la luz.

Man of every street
of dawn
towering heaps of failures
statue of my homeland
sculpted from the deep roots of night.
Take my hand
and we'll listen together
how the river of lavender awakens to sing
and the broken shouts announce the light.

NOS REFUGIAMOS

Nos refugiamos bajo la sombra de la palabra herida
fluyendo desde su llaga como savia bienhechora.
Hicimos de nosotros la vida mutilada
y aprendimos a remover la tierra
buscando las raíces del amor.

La tarde había llegado con su paso lento.
Mientras cigarras preludiaban la llegada de su sombra
pequeñas estrellas diseminadas en la yerba
iluminaron su arribo.
Sólo los corazones aferrados a la tierra
se irguieron sobre el silencio,
se nutrieron de su fatiga
y hablaron a través del viento
de su vida arribada.

Por las calles anduvo nuestra mirada ida,
Algún corazón temblando presintió nuestra presencia
y huimos de la vida que se nos ofrecía
desde aquellas manos y ojos y palabras
sin que la huella quedara de nuestro paso.

Nocturnas hilanderas cubrieron nuestro recuerdo;
de nosotros no quedaría más que nuestra voz:
Hombre, ¡he aquí tu rastro!
Mujer, he aquí el espejo que poseyera tu rostro.
Joven corajudo ¡Oh pobre muchacho!
no dejaste tu semen frutecido en la tierra.

WE TAKE REFUGE

We take refuge in the wounded word's shadow
flowing from your sore like a healing sap.
We made from ourselves this mutilated life
and learned to move the earth
searching for the roots of love.

Evening arrived slowly.
While cicadas preface the coming night
tiny stars extinguish in the grass
illuminating your arrival.
Only hearts that cling to the earth
stand over silence,
are nourished from fatigue
and speak following the wind
of your arriving life.

Our gone gaze wandered through the streets.
Some trembling heart sensed us,
we fled from the life offered us
from those hands and eyes and words
without leaving any footprints.

Nocturnal silk spinners obscure our memories;
they want nothing else from us but our voices:
Man, here is your trail.
Woman, here is the mirror possessing your face.
Courageous youth, poor child,
you left no life on this earth.

No importa,
yo me declaro tu hijo
y en tu nombre elevaré mi voz
y en mi nombre guardarás silencio
porque yo prolongaré tu grito y tu mirada
y no tendrás olvido,
porque en tu nombre estaré llorando,
sonriendo
hasta que fluya de la palabra herida mi sangre
que adoptará tu nombre.
Nos refugiamos bajo las sombras distraídas de los árboles
y desde ellas
corrimos al encuentro de la vida mutilada,
removimos la tierra
y encontramos las raíces del amor
profundamente arraigadas al corazón de nuestros muertos.

It doesn't matter,
I declare myself your son
and in your name I'll raise my voice
and in my name you guard the silence
I will prolong your shout and your stare,
and you won't be forgotten,
because in your name I will be crying,
smiling
until my blood flows from the wounded word
that will adopt your name.
We take refuge in the distracted shadows of trees
and from them
we run toward this mutilated life,
we moved the earth
and found the roots of love
ingrained deeply in the hearts of our dead.

PATRIA

Patria
he sentido cómo desde tu hambrienta latitud
sube mi pueblo a través de sonoras esencias
y palpables respiraciones.

Patria
he sentido como corres a través de mi sangre
agolpándote en mi garganta
golpeándome la nuca
acudiendo a gritos a mi canto.
He presenciado desde lejos tu angustia
crecida en la copa de los árboles
explotando en los frutos
en las aves migratorias
que habitan tu desnuda extensión de lágrima caída.

He escuchado tu voz
levantada por el aroma de mi llanto
y de mi sudor
del sudor del campesino y del obrero
talados como viejos pinares montañeses.

Te he visto correr sobre las mejillas de nuestras jóvenes
luchadoras
hallando la forma definitiva de la muerte.
He escuchado tu grito madre de niños tísicos
tísica tú misma
madre fecunda
pauperada por los que te roban el aluminio limpio
como lágrimas de niño
y disuelven el acero de tus entrañas
en las intensas ascuas del odio
el robo y el crimen de reyezuelos a sueldo.

HOMELAND

Homeland
from your starved latitude I felt
my people rise through sonorous essences
and heavy breaths.

Homeland
I felt how you grip through my blood
squeezing my throat
bruising my neck
screaming along to my song.
I witnessed your anguish from afar
blooming in treetops
erupting from fruit,
in fleeing birds
inhabiting your blank expanse of fallen tears.

I heard your voice
lift on the scent of my cry
and my sweat
the sweat of a peasant worker
cut down like old mountain pines.

I saw you streak across the cheeks of children
fighters
finding death's final form.
I heard your mothered call with withered children
you yourself withered
fertile mother
impoverished by those stealing your bright ores
like children's tears
and dissolving the steel of your bowels
in the intense embers of hatred
thieves funded by kings.

Oh patria
mi patria
cada vez que pronuncio tu nombre
se abre una herida en mi corazón
y desde allí tus ojos me miran
y miran al mundo
y miran a América
a las Antillas divididas por el dollar
al bracero manco por el dollar
a la mujer destrozada en los arrabales
o en los prostíbulos
también por el dollar,
que arriba a nuestras playas vestido de lino
en grandes maletas grises
catafalcos enormes que traen a nuestra América
junto a las sonrisas ensayadas,
la muerte.

Oh patria
girón de sangre
desde el centro del llanto
te espero
te escucho
y te canto.

Quizás Patria mía
estás pensando en mí
en mi amigo Juan o en Pablo
caídos por ti
cercenados
sobre la amarilla sonrisa de los maizales
donde el sol se multiplica en granos.

Lloras, Patria,
sangras, sufres,
pero nosotros
desnudos, estamos construyendo a cada minuto
él advenimiento terrible de la justicia.

Oh homeland
my homeland
every time I speak your name
a fissure forms in my heart
and from its depths your eyes stare back
and see the world
and see America
the Antilles divided by the dollar
the one-armed man working for the dollar
the woman shattered in the suburbs
or brothels
for the dollar,
and up on our beaches dressed in linen
laid in large gray luggage
atop giant biers bringing our America
together with rehearsed smiles:
the dead.

Oh homeland
bloody pennant
from the screaming center
I await you
I hear you
I sing.

Maybe you, my homeland,
are thinking of me
of my friend Juan or Pablo
who died for you
severed
in the yellow grimace of the cornfield
where the sun multiplies in every grain.

My homeland, crying,
bleeding, suffering,
but we
are bare, every minute building
toward the terrible advent of justice.

Lloras, Patria,
pero no tardaremos en destruir las cuerdas que atan tu canto.
Incendiaremos con un fuego nuevo
que crece y seguirá creciendo
sobre las magulladuras del torso campesino
donde el Sol siempre a sus espaldas cayendo
descansa.

Oh patria
crecerás
estarás creciendo ya.

El hambre del pueblo
el odio del pueblo
tornado grito y cólera sed insaciable
estremecimiento terrible del orbe
caída irremisible del dollar
reconstruirá lentamente
grano a grano
cada mazorca robada a nuestra esperanza.

Patria,
los que no han nacido
nosotros los que hemos nacido y crecemos
y volvemos a nacer y a crecer
siempre
a cada minuto
hacha, palo y pico
cuchillo y garrote en nuestras manos
sin ninguna indumentaria
desnudos
trocaremos la vegetación
haremos de esta tierra
nuestra tierra
morada del trabajo y la justicia
canto de prole vegetal, mineral y humana
hollando la faz de la tierra antillana
hoy cadalso del hombre caribe.

My homeland, crying,
but soon we'll cut the cords that constrain your song.
We'll burn with a new fire
that grows and keeps growing
over the laborers' bruised backs
where the sun that leans into them
comes to rest.

Oh homeland
you'll grow
you're growing.

The town's hunger
the town's hatred
a tornado of shouts and angry insatiable thirst
terrible shuddering of this world
fall of the unforgiving dollar
slowly rebuilding
grain by grain
every stolen stalk of hope.

Homeland,
those still unborn
those of us born and growing
and continue to be born and grow
always
every minute—
hatchet, stick, and pickaxe
knives and clubs in our fists
without cloths
naked
charging through the trees—
will make our land
of this land
a home for work and justice
song of nature, stone, and humanity
treading the Antillean earth
scaffold of the Caribbean.

A UN LÍDER NEGRO ASESINADO

Todas las sombras blancas se conjuraron
para matar un negro.
Todo si vigor negro se levantó
para llevar sobre sus hombros al negro asesinado.
Mataron un negro desde los tejados del Sur,
desde el algodón del Sur
bajo un sol amordazado.
Mataron a un hombre negro.
Fragmentaron el óvulo fecundado por Abraham Lincoln
en el mutilado corazón del Mississipi.
Despedazaron la aurora
y miles de gritos rompieron los cristales cotidianos de
Norteamérica.
Los negros protestaban rugían
estremecían de norte a sur la dilatada extensión agreste del odio
estrellándose en el rostro de los verdugos.
En el Sur cundieron los garrotes
mientras la multitud negra cargaba un cadáver agujereado
donde la luz se filtraba despertando la sangre.
Destrozaron un pedazo de vigor negro.
Desde un tejado
horadaron el torso del amor.
El hombre cayó
cayó la esperanza
los días
las horas y los minutos enmudecieron
hablaron los patíbulos
las calles acumularon muerte,
ladrillos, piedras, sangre,
sangre de negro
sangre del Sur
sangre de Norteamérica

FOR AN ASSASSINATED BLACK LEADER

All the white shadows were conjured
to kill a Black man.
All the black vigor rose
to carry the murdered black man on its shoulders.
They killed a Black man from the roofs of the South,
from the cotton of the South
under the gagging sun.
They killed a Black man.
They fractured Lincoln's unborn ideals
in the mutilated heart of Mississippi,
shredded the dawn
and a thousand shouts tore the daily crystals of
America.
Roaring black protest
shaking from north to south the wild dilated country of hate,
striking the executioner's face.
In the South billy clubs were handed out
while the black multitude carried the kept body
where filtered light awakens the blood.
They destroyed a piece of black vigor.
From a roof
they pierced his living body.
The man fell
hope fell
the days
the hours and minutes froze
the gallows spoke
the streets filled with death,
bricks, rocks, blood,
black blood
blood of the South
blood of America.

Medgar Evers
yace en el fondo del útero primero
sonriendo
destilando el agua de los ríos
las voces de los matorrales
y el grito que rebota contra las montañas ceñudas
abriendo cavidades en el corazón de arcilla de Whitman
o en el torso de dulce granito de Lincoln
en cuya muerte parida
duerme una paloma con crías negras y blancas.
Cayó
armado por la ternura
simple como el maíz
que va sorbiendo el sol hasta ser una mazorca de luz.
Cayó Medgar
mientras desgranaba su luminosa mazorca
desbordando amor por todo lo que habita desde siempre.
Mataron un negro.
Un clamor aceraba la geografía
el Sur crujía bajo la marcha negra
que atronaba desde el cementerio
destruyendo barreras de perros y matones
de fuego derramándose.
Han pasado muchos días.
El negro muerto del Sur
no ha cesado de palpitar
agitando el algodón del Sur
incendiando el aire de Birmingham
quebrando las alambradas de Jackson
amamantando la esperanza.
Asesinaron un negro.

Medgar Evers
lies in the first womb
looking out
distilling the river's water
the shrubberies' voices
and the shouts that bounce off the frowning mountains
opening cavities in the heart of Whitman's earth
or in the granite torso of Lincoln
in whose death we were born
where a dove sleeps with its black and white offspring.
Felled
armed with tenderness
true as maize
absorbing sunshine until it's a stalk of light.
Medgar fell
shedding luminous leaves
overflowing over everything.
They murdered a Black man.
Fury paved the landscape
the South crunched under the black march
that thundered from the cemetery
destroying barricades of dogs and thug cops
of spilling fire.
Many days have passed.
The dead Black man of the South
has not ceased fluttering
agitating the Southern cotton
incinerating the Birmingham air
tearing the barbed wire of Jackson
feeding hope.
They assassinated a Black man.

Miles de negros nacieron a la lucha
esgrimieron una hoz de llanto
y marcharon hacia las cadenas
de odio y terror desatado
hacia la luz arrancada de sus ojos
hacia la canción arrebatada de sus labios.
Marchaban los negros
hombres, mujeres y niños
estudiantes leyendo la alborada
obreros
ancianos exprimiendo el siglo
marchaban cantando.
Medgar Evers
Desde su tumba acorazaba la cólera negra
cayendo sobre la garra blanca
sobre el odio blanco
sobre el patíbulo blanco
mientras en su boca llena de tierra
crecían los lirios.
Cayó Medgar
fue un día de niños coreando la canción del abuelo John
de niñas zurciendo las roturas de la luz
cayó un negro
una esperanza
una lágrima.
El reloj asesinaba el tiempo
había luz, mucha luz
en las gargantas que amasaban la canción
en las manos que hacían parir las rocas aullando.
Medgar Evers cayó.
Fue negro
fue esperanza
fue hombre.

Thousands of children born into this fight
wielding a scythe of tears
marching toward the chains
of hate and terror undone
toward the light torn from his eyes
toward the song ripped from his lips.
Marching
men, women, children,
students reading the dawn
labourers,
the elderly holding tight to the century
marching and singing.
Medgar Evers
from the grave armed the black anger
slamming it over the white claw
over the white hate
over the white gallows
while in his dirt-filled mouth
grow lilies.
Medgar fell
on a day of boys singing their grandfathers' songs
of girls mending cracks in light
a Black man fell
a hope
a tear.
The clock murdered time
and there was light, so much light
in the throats that knead the songs
in the hands that birthed those howling rocks.
Medgar Evers fell.
He was black
he was hope
he was man.

Cayó el negro
cayó la esperanza
cayó el hombre.
Se irguieron los fusiles
el fuego y las ballonetas
la sangre pavimentó las rutas del Sur
El Mississipi arrastró la canción destrozada.
Oh Mississippi
llanto del Sur
llanto de los negros
llanto de Norteamérica.
Jackson
féretro
tumba
silencio.
Oh Mississippi
sol maduro
lucha
Oh Norteamérica
argamasa
con montones de linchados esperando.

A Black man was felled
hope was felled
man was felled.
Rifles were raised
fire and bayonets
blood paves the Southern roads
the Mississippi drags its tattered song.
Oh Mississippi
Southern cry
black cry
American cry.
Jackson
coffin
tomb
silence.
Oh Mississippi
ripe sun
fight
Oh America,
concrete
heaps of the unlynched.

LA MUERTE

I

En cada rincón
la muerte.
En cada terrón
la muerte.
En cada palabra
la muerte.
En cada lote de silencio
la muerte.
En cada amanecer
a muerte.
La arcilla y el granito gimieron,
los ríos y los charcos gritaron,
los vegetales sombríos
derramaron su savia y tomaron la sangre que vagaba.

Cada hoja se hizo palabra,
cada piedra,
dura hechura del amor,
cada parcela tumba corajuda.

Los guerrilleros alzados
abrieron los párpados de la piedra
y desde allí alimentaron los surcos
y el agua humedeció sus palabras
lavó sus nombres como si fuesen semillas.

THE DEAD

I

In every corner
the dead.
In every lump of dirt
the dead.
In every word
the dead.
In each allotment of silence
the dead.
Every morning
the dead.
The clay and granite moan,
the rivers and puddles shout,
the shaded plants
spill their sap and drink the wandering blood.

Every leaf turns into a word,
every rock,
love's hard work,
every courageous tomb.

The guerrilla fighters
part the rock's eyelids
and feed the furrows,
the water dampens their words
washing their names like seeds.

Allí, en lo alto de la tierra,
en las Manaclas levantaron su tienda.
Allí, bajo el techo vegetal del amor se cobijaron
y sólo la brisa supo de ellos,
de la mancha de su sangre por las agrietadas soledades.

Allí aprendieron a trepar como lianas por el aire,
y supieron reconocer
el fatigado temblor del útero de piedra
mientras componía sus criaturas
bajo las soledades celestes.

Allí averiguaron el lenguaje de las hojas,
aprendieron el grito de la tierra
cuando la habitan los hombres de la pradera,
el sonido desatado de las ciudades
libre de cenizas y de polvo.

Allí levantaron su tienda
abrazaron el duro perfil de la noche
sin que el pueblo viera la ronda de la muerte
sobre la morada del hombre,
sobre la desnuda morada de la gente guerrillera.

¡Ay! Quisiera que mi voz fuese sonora como las suyas,
que mis ojos habitaran el espacio donde habitaron y cayeron
los que escalaban las estrellas
y hacían sangrar la dura roca,
hablar al duro silencio de las Manaclas.

There, atop the earth
on the Manaclas Mountains, they raised their tents.
There, under adoring treetops, they took shelter
only the wind knew,
stained blood on cracked loneliness.

There they learned to climb like vines through the air,
learned to recognize
the trembling fatigue of the stone womb
while composing creatures
below the celestial solitude.

There they learned the language of leaves,
learned the earth's cry
the prairie men inhabit,
wild city sounds
free of ash and dust.

There they raised their tents
embracing night's hard outline
without the people seeing death's rounds
over the towns,
over the guerrillas' open dwellings.

Oh! If only my voice rang like theirs,
my eyes housed in the space where they lived and died,
those who climbed the stars
and bleed the hard stones,
to speak to the hard silence of the Manaclas.

Si pudiera seguir sus pisadas,
detenerme en cada huella,
recoger cada pedazo de lienzo verde,
cada palabra,
cada mensaje de lodo o granito,
cada silencio de sangre
y soledades rotas
tendría en mis manos la savia primera,
la voz de las soledades,
adentrándose en los oídos y los ojos de la gente guerrillera.
Si no estuve allí,
¿qué podré decir?
Si no vi su sangre alimentar los bosques,
¿qué diré?
Si no supe de sus caminatas,
de sus noches de amor con el viento y la piedra
¿cómo reconocer su prole de lianas y granito y lodo?

Se alzaron,
abrieron sus pechos y la Patria habitó en sus entrañas,
su sangre corrió y en la patria habitaron.

Y yo desde esta pradera ahora sin nombre,
en medio de estas calles anónimas
voy reconstruyendo
con fragmentos de soledad y silencio cada paso;
cada palabra,
cada momento en que el hombre y la tierra se aparearon.

If I could follow their footsteps,
stop in each tread,
pick up every piece of green cloth,
every word,
every message made of mud or granite,
every bloodied silence
and broken solitude,
I would hold in my hand the original life,
that solitude's voice,
entering the ears and eyes of the guerrillas.
If one wasn't there,
what can they say?
If I didn't see their blood feeding the forest,
what would I say?
If I didn't know their routes,
of their nights spent under the wind and rocks,
how would I recognize their children of vines and granite and mud?

They rose,
opened their bellies, and our homeland entered their entrails,
their blood ran through the homeland within them.

And from this now nameless meadow,
in the middle of these anonymous streets,
I go, reconstructing
with fragments of solitude and silence in each step;
every word,
every moment where men and earth appeared.

II

Iré por entre las piedras,
hablaré con los vegetales
me alimentaré de raíces nuevas,
ellos me dirán la historia,
me mostrarán el rostro del amor,
la estatura frustrada de la infancia,
Porque decidme si no eran la infancia del mundo,
explicadme, ¿qué es el amor,
dónde habita la infancia?

III

Levantaron sus voces por defender la Patria
porque ella expiraba
su sangre derramada,
y sus hijos asesinados.

Se alzaron a los montes
a salvar lo que de ella quedaba,
el tejido vegetal de la vida quisqueyana,
su pecho ancho
de piedra virgen y mármol ciego.

II

I'll go through the rocks,
I'll speak with the trees,
I'll feed on new roots,
they'll tell me the history,
they'll show me love's face,
the frustrated stature of innocence,
because if you tell me this isn't the earth's childhood
then explain, what is love?
Where does innocence live?

III

They raised their voices to defend their homeland
because she was dying
from so much spilled blood
from her assassin sons.

They rose to the mountains
to save what was left of her,
the green skin of Quisqueyana life,
her belly wide with
virgin rocks and blind marble.

EN LA NOCHE

Y luego, en la noche, mirar hacia el vacío,
hablar,
buscar los hombros de la mujer,
aspirar el aire,
contemplar vagamente los astros,
que han observado las edades del mundo
y sentirse más cerca, parte de la tierra.

HERMANO desplomado sobre esta pequeña isla
en nombre de tus lágrimas
y en nombre de tus versos.
Ahora la ciudad no tiene tu sonrisa
ni tu palabra como de humo.
Ahora la ciudad no tiene tus pasos
ni tus ojos la luz y las gaviotas cuyo vuelo es la altura de la dicha.

Hermano cerca de nosotros por la raíz de tu canto.
Hermano cerca por tu forma de entrada a la tierra.
¡Tu sangre en el obús jamás se borrará!
Ahora no tienes los álamos ni los niños,
la tarde ni el mar fosforescente de algas.
Ahora no tienes las muchachas perdidas
ni las madres como surcos.
Ahora no tienes ni camisas
ni libros.
Ahora te repartes.

IN THE NIGHT

And then, in the night, look into the void,
speak,
seek a woman's shoulder,
aspire to be air,
vaguely contemplate the stars,
who've watched the world age
and feel closer, part of the earth.

Brother, collapsed on this small island
in the name of your tears
and in the name of your poems.
Now the city misses your smile
and your words like smoke.
Now the city misses your footprints
and your eyes of light and the seagulls who fly as high as joy.

Brother, close to us by the roots of your song.
Brother, close by your entryway into the earth.
Your blood staining the bombshell will never wash away.
Now you have neither the trees nor the children,
not the evenings nor the sea glowing with algae.
Now you have neither the lost girls
nor the furrowed mothers.
Now you don't even have shirts
or books.
Now you're shared.

WALT WHITMAN

Señores
Walt Whitman.
corazón ancho,
barba inmensa,
ha vuelto.
Ha vuelto timoneando la palabra
sobre un mar de palabras.
Nos lo trajo Pedro
también capitán de la palabra
sobre un mar de palabras amortajadas.

Nos lo trajo envuelto en auroras,
destrozado por la ausencia y la espera.
Walt Whitman y su barba cósmica,
Walt Whitman
y sus brazos reconstruidos por la palabra,
recamados en cada obrero y su canción
desde el llanto incontenible de las Antillas.
Volvió con su barba transparente,
inmensa,
hecha sangre,
con su garganta hecha grito desgarrado,
con sus manos enormes
donde América cobijara su cabeza,
su llanto,
su esperanza,
sangrando.

Volvió con Pedro,
a través de Pedro,
desde el llanto,
desde la sangre que corre por mi tierra,
desde las minas,
las cordilleras,

WALT WHITMAN

Sirs
Walt Whitman,
wide heart,
immense beard,
has returned.
You've returned guiding the word
over a sea of words.
Saint Peter brought you to us,
fellow captain of the word,
over a sea of shrouded words.

You were brought to us enveloped in auroras,
shattered by absence and waiting.
Walt Whitman and your cosmic beard,
Walt Whitman
and your arms rebuilt by words,
embroidered in every work and song
from the irrepressible cry of the Antilles.
Returned with your transparent beard,
immense,
made of blood,
with your shout-torn throat,
with your enormous hands
where America shelters your head,
your cry,
your hope,
bleeding.

You returned with Saint Peter,
after Saint Peter,
from the cry,
from the blood running through my earth,
from the mines,
the mountains,

volvió a través de Pedro,
a través de sus palabras nacidas en las canteras,
cargadas de partidas,
azotando los vientos,
tiñéndose de rojo con mi sangre,
con la sangre de los mineros,
de los cañaverales.
Volvió a través de Pedro,
de las cruces que crecen en el alma.

Volvió Walt Whitman,
un cosmos,
hijo de Manhattan,
nos lo trajo Pedro
desde su corazón azotado por el llanto,
por la sangre de América,
de esta América que cobijara una barba cósmica
de un hijo de Manhattan.

¡Oh, Walt Whitman
un cosmos,
hijo de Manhattan,
tu voz vuelve a ser nuestra:
la redimió Pedro,
a hurtadillas la robó de los bancos,
de los trusts,
las corporaciones
y limpió con sus dedos tu barba hecha de auroras
para que azotara mi isla,
nuestra isla.
Has vuelto a nosotros, viejo barbudo,
a nosotros los herreros,
a nosotros los explotados,
has vuelto con tu voz restituida al llanto
y a la esperanza;
desde el silencio retornada
por una voz que sabe a sangre y a azúcar.

you returned after Saint Peter,
behind your words born in quarries,
pieced together,
lashing the winds,
dying red with my blood,
with the blood of my miners,
from the cane fields.
You returned after Saint Peter,
from crosses that grow in the soul.

Walt Whitman returned,
a cosmos,
son of Manhattan,
brought to us by Saint Peter,
from his shout-torn heart,
from the blood of America,
from this America housing the cosmic beard
of a son of Manhattan.

Oh, Walt Whitman
a cosmos,
son of Manhattan,
your voice returns to us:
redeemed by Saint Peter,
quietly stolen from the banks,
from the trusts,
from the corporations,
who cleaned that auroral beard with his fingers
to lash my island,
our island.
You've returned to us, old beard,
to us, the blacksmiths,
to us, the exploited,
you've returned with your voice restoring the cry
and hope;
returned from the silence
a voice that tastes of sugar and blood.

¡Oh, Walt Whitman
restituido al llanto,
al amor,
a nuestros mozalbetes
restituido desde la sombra,
a nuestras montañas,
a nuestros ríos,
a los llaneros,
a los gauchos,
a los mineros del Norte
por Pedro,
con la sangre de los mineros,
de los cañaverales.
volvió a través de Pedro,
de las cruces que crecen en el alma.

Volvió Walt Whitman,
un cosmos,
hijo de Manhattan,
nos lo trajo Pedro
desde su corazón azotado por el llanto,
por la sangre de América,
de esta América que cobijara una barba cósmica
de un hijo de Manhattan.

¡Oh, Walt Whitman
un cosmos,
hijo de Manhattan,
tu voz vuelve a ser nuestra:
la redimió Pedro,
a hurtadillas la robó de los bancos,
de los trusts,
las corporaciones
y limpió con sus dedos tu barba hecha de auroras
para que azotara mi isla,
nuestra isla.

Oh, Walt Whitman
restored the cry,
the love,
our young men,
restored from the shadows,
our mountains,
our rivers,
our plainsmen,
our cowboys,
our miners in the north,
for Saint Peter,
with the blood of the miners,
from the cane fields.
You returned after Saint Peter,
from the crosses that grow in the soul.

You've returned, Walt Whitman,
a cosmos,
son of Manhattan,
brought to us by Saint Peter
from his shout-torn heart,
for the blood of America,
from this America housing the cosmic beard
of a son of Manhattan.

Oh, Walt Whitman
a cosmos,
son of Manhattan,
your voice brought back to us:
Saint Peter redeemed it,
quietly stolen from the banks,
from the trusts,
corporations,
who cleaned that auroral beard with his fingers
to lash my island,
our island.

Has vuelto a nosotros, viejo barbudo,
a nosotros los herreros,
a nosotros los explotados,
has vuelto con tu voz restituida al llanto
y a la esperanza;
desde el silencio retornada
por una voz que sabe a sangre y a azúcar.

¡Oh, Walt Whitman
restituido al llanto,
al amor,
a nuestros mozalbetes
restituido desde la sombra,
a nuestras montañas,
a nuestros ríos,
a los llaneros,
a los gauchos,
a los mineros del Norte
por Pedro,
forjador de soles,
enfermo de auroras,
que destila de las rocas, como tú,
amor,
de la espera
amor,
de la sangre derramada
vida,
¡Oh, Walt Whitman,
un cosmos,
hijo de Manhattan,
restituido a nosotros desde el silencio
por Pedro,
otros cosmos
hijo del Caribe.

You've returned to us, old beard,
to us, the blacksmiths,
to us, the exploited,
you've returned with your voice restoring the cry
and hope;
returned from the silence
a voice that tastes of sugar and blood.

Oh, Walt Whitman
restored the cry,
the love,
our young men,
restored from the shadows,
our mountains,
our rivers,
our plainsmen,
our cowboys,
our miners in the north,
for Saint Peter,
forged from stars,
fevered by auroras,
that distills from the rocks, like you,
love,
from longing
love,
from spilled blood
life,
Oh, Walt Whitman,
a cosmos,
son of Manhattan,
restored to us from the silence
by Saint Peter,
another cosmos,
son of the Caribbean.

CANTO A AMÉRICA

América sentada sobre los hombros de la noche
contando los rostros del hambre
descifrando el lenguaje de la tristeza
y midiendo las modulaciones del odio en el vientre de nuestros
hijos
América te han robado la alegría
destruyeron los maseteros de tu rostro
y ataron tu corazón a la vigilia
donde deambulan millones de seres
habitados por la muerte,
por una muerte que arrastramos desde que el hombre de allende
sembró su espada antes que su nombre en esta tierra.
y la mugre
y el moho
y el fango
en nuestra vida de sol desgranado.

América levántate América
sacude el polvo y el moho acumulados en ti.
América renace
renace América
hombres americanos
mujeres y jóvenes de América
escuchad el temblor que sacude las Antillas
del pico en la piedra naciendo
la voz de un niño que canta desde una pequeña Isla
del martillo sobre el andamio
cuyos hombros construyen a golpe de carcajadas
y de coraje
el orbe puro del "Amor Americano".

SONG FOR AMERICA

America, sitting atop the night's shoulders
singing in the faces of the hungry
deciphering the language of sadness
measuring the modulation of hatred in our children's
stomachs.
America, they've stolen your joy
destroying the muscles in your face
tied your heart to the vigil
where thousands of beings wander
inhabited by death,
a death we drag since man, from beyond,
buried his sword, before your name on this earth.
And the dirt
and the mold
and the mud
of our sun-threshed life.

America, get up America
shake off the dust and rust inside you.
America reborn
reborn America
American men
American women and children
listen to the tremor rumbling from the Antilles
from that stone peak giving birth
to the voice of a child singing from a tiny island
from the hammering of the scaffold
whose shoulders are built from the blows of cackles
and courage
the pure orb of "American love."

Escuchad
un nuevo grito infla el velamen de América
arrastrada por los enemigos del hombre
mercaderes
apoderados de los templos y las Biblias
en los juzgados de paz y de muerte
para que la verdad no incendie a Bolivia sedienta,
estrangulada por un cordón de arcilla
al heredero del Inca
muerto en una hoguera que no se ha extinguido aún
para que la luz no acaricie el quetzal dormido
sobre las ruinas del silencio aborigen,
a Chile, larga, vibrante,
como una lanza clavada en el corazón de un araucano;
a Centroamérica
masacrada con bananas dinamitadas,
a Venezuela
donde el Capital tiene su más empinado patíbulo
y las huestes del amor un bastión inexpugnable.
Al Brasil con muchas tierras y pocos habitantes
adornados sus andrajos de diamantes.
y con muchas lágrimas en la solapa de los militares
mientras que en Argentina y en Paraguay
los coágulos adornan los trofeos de los comandantes
y por las chimeneas sube un olor a carne machacada.
Oh América!
ahora sin velamen
sin brújula
recodo del hambre
amargo sabor de fruta nueva caída del árbol
sin sombra
bajo cuya derruida arquitectura
el hombre americano lame el dorso de la tristeza.

Listen
a new howl fills the sails of America
dragged by the enemies of man
capitalists
proxies of the temples and Bibles
in the courts of peace and death
so the truth does not burn Bolivia into thirst,
strangled with a clay cord
the heir of the Incas
dead on an eternal bonfire
so the light won't awaken the sleeping quetzal
atop the ruins of aboriginal silence,
to Chile, long and vibrant,
a spear pierced through the heart of an Araucanian;
to Central America
massacred by dynamited bananas,
to Venezuela
where the capital houses their steepest gallows
and the hosts of love are an impenetrable bastion.
To Brazil with large land and few people
adorning their rags with diamonds
tears on the soldiers lapels
while in Argentina and Paraguay
blood clots hang from the commanders' medals
and from chimneys rise the stench of crushed meat.
Oh America!
Now without sail
without compass
bent from hunger
bitter fruit fallen
from a shadeless tree
under whose ruined structure
the American licks the back of sadness.

¡Oh América!
pedazo de llanto disecado,
América, América,
renace América
hombres esclavizados de América
encended las hogueras
y marchad hacia la luz que guarda la historia para vosotros.

Marchad
herederos de la sangre
llaneros colombianos
con vuestros pechos enormes
donde florecen los girasoles.
Indios del Perú
y del Ecuador adormecidos con coca
alzad la frente antigua de la pureza
y decid vuestro secreto.

Y tú Puerto Rico
enclavada en las mismas fauces del odio
pequeño terrón de azúcar plagado de alimañas
asesinada lentamente
entre agobiantes moles de hierro y vidrio.
Oh Puerto Rico
te amo más que a ninguna otra patria americana
porque habitas perennemente el llanto
te amo
te amo
te amo desde Santo Domingo
cuerpo desmembrado
grito partido en dos
pero nacido de una sola garganta
de una misma angustia,
sola.

Oh America!
Piece of the dissected chant,
America, America,
reborn America
burdened men of America
light your bonfires
and march toward the light that guards history.

March
inheritors of blood
Colombian cowboys
with their enormous stomachs
where sunflowers bloom.
Natives of Peru
and Ecuador sleepy with coca
raise the ancient face of purity
and tell your secrets.

And you, Puerto Rico,
nailed to the jaws of hatred
small lump of sugar plagued by vermin
slow assassination
crushed between masses of metal and glass.
Oh Puerto Rico,
I love you more than any other American homeland
because you permanently inhabit the cry
I love you
I love you
I love you from Santo Domingo
dismembered corpse
shout parted in two
but born of a single throat
from a single anguish,
alone.

Oh América
pedazo de llanto disecado
con un mañana luminoso
que construyen los guerrilleros del amor
que tienen en Cuba su sonrisa más amplia.

Oh América
por ti luchan muchos hombres
por ti mueren
y cuánto amor es preciso albergar
para morir por ti
por una América que no ha nacido aún
y que tardará todavía por nacer.
Americanos del nuevo Evangelio
sostened con vuestras manos
el clamor de nuestros corazones
alzad bien alto nuestro grito
apretad bien los nudos que nos atan a la ternura
el alba infantil de la sonrisa
atadla con vuestras venas
mojadla con vuestra sangre
purificadla con vuestro llanto.

Americanos del nuevo Evangelio
alzad bien alto nuestro grito
que sea lo único que el diluvio no ahogue
porque de él nacerán las generaciones de la alegría
el hombre amplio
tan amplio como la sonrisa de la proletaria alba
ebrio siempre de vigor
de amor que se derrama
mientras edifica la vida
sobre los escombros de la vida pasada.

Oh America
piece of the dissected chant
with a luminous morning
built by the guerillas of love
who have their widest smile in Cuba.

Oh America
for you so many men fight
for you they die
how much love must be housed
to die for you
for an America not yet born
and won't be for some time.
Americans of the new gospel
hold in your hands
our heart's clamor
raise high our cry
tighten the knots that tie us to tenderness
the infant dawn of a smile
tied with your veins
wet with your blood
purified by your cry.

Americans of the new gospel
raise high our cry
so it survives the flood
because it will give birth to generations of happiness
an ample mankind
large as the smile of the proletarian sunrise
forever seedlings of vigor
of spilled love
while life edifies
over the debris of a past life.

Americanos del año 63 de este siglo
evangelizadores del nuevo mundo
alzad la frente
alzadla bien alto
para que veáis de lejos la tierra que constituye nuestra prole
futura.
con nuestros restos:
con nuestras manos y nuestros huesos
con nuestros órganos,
con todo nuestro ser,
con esta vida de agobios,
hecha para sobrevivirse
vedla
y no desfallezcáis
porque vosotros sois la lumbre de mañana
la niñez eterna
el gesto infantil de los que aman
dándolo todo
recibiéndolo todo
por esta vida nuestra sumergida en sus voces.

Americans of 1963, of this century,
evangelizers of the new world
raise your heads
raise them high
to see from afar this land that constitutes
our future.
With our remains:
with our hands and bones
with our organs,
with all our being,
with this burdened life,
built to survive,
see it
and do not faint
because we are tomorrow's fire
the eternal youth
the gesture of those who love
giving everything
taking everything
for this life submerged in your voices.

LLEGASTE

Con tu andar de carbón humedecido
llegaste a través del viento
que viola mi ventana.

Llegaste cargada de transparencias
a través de la brisa matinal
en medio de una lucha interminable
entre los que marchan y los que quedan.

Llegaste a través de la mañana hendida por el canto del gallo.
Penetraste en mi casa edificada con llanto
con piedras habitadas por algas
y lagartos sorprendidos entre las grietas.
Venías de no sé qué riberas,
hablaste de cosas que no han sido;
eres algo así, como un presentimiento
pesado, casi palpable, material.

Hablaste de un vegetal sombrío
de ondulantes y largos brazos
que crece estrangulando sueños
bajo las aguas
bajo los techos heridos
bajo los pies descalzos de la miseria.

Tu presencia me la hizo sentir
el húmedo silencio que destilaba mi alcoba
el salino perfume que me cubría de escamas
y el lento taconeo de tu marcha
detenida en un presente sin límites.

YOU ARRIVED

With your humid charcoal walk
you arrived through the wind
that rattles my window.

You arrived full of transparencies
on the morning breeze
in the middle of an endless fight
between those who march and those who stay.

You arrived in the morning cleaved by the rooster's call.
You entered my home built with cries
with moss-covered rocks
and surprised lizards in the cracks.
You came from unknown riverbanks,
you spoke of things that have yet to happen;
you are something like that, a heavy
premonition, almost manifested.

You spoke of a somber plant
of long billowing arms
that grow to strangle dreams
beneath the water
beneath decaying roofs
beneath the bare feet of misery.

Your presence made me feel
the humid silence distilling my room
salted perfume covering me in scales
and the slow tapping of a march
detained in a limitless present.

Venías de las aguas de un mar desconocido
tu presencia era algo mío que estrangulara de olvido
que matara el tiempo con sus largos dedos descalcificados.
Viniste, dijiste muchas cosas
y sin embargo no pronunciaste palabra alguna
nos amamos y sin embargo no nos tocamos,
no pude verte... pero estabas ahí
detenida en un minuto que no te pertenecía;
con tu aliento tapiado por el aliento de flores caídas
en el terrible presente de los estanques.
No pude verte... pero estabas allí,
me amaste y sin embargo no nos tocamos.
Dijimos muchas cosas en un abecedario tejido de silencio
bajo un campanario destrozado.

Te adentraste en mi ser
perforando mi aliento con tu cortante aliento
exprimiste la fuente de mi llanto
y en mi llanto lavaste tu cuerpo del silencio
de la soledad de tu mundo
del presente interminable de tu vida;
luego te marchaste
abriendo los párpados cerrados de mi ventana
asida de las nubes.

Abajo la ciudad y sus fantasmas;
sus vivos muriendo lentamente
entre alcoholes y mentiras que endulzan la partida
hacia el silencio
tapiado por algas ahogando lagartos,
destrozando peces dormidos
cubriendo lentamente la tierra de moho

You came from the waters of an unknown sea
your presence was something mine strangled from oblivion
that will murder time with its huge decalcified fingers.
You came, said many things
but didn't pronounce a single word
we love one another and yet never touched,
I could not see you, but you were there
detained in a moment that did not belong to you;
with your breath walled off by the breath of fallen flowers
in the terrible presence of water.
I could not see you, but you were there,
you loved me and yet we never touched.
We said many things in a language weaved from silence
under a toppled bell tower.

You entered my being
perforating my breath with your piercing breath
wringing the fountain of my cry
and under my cry you washed your body of silence
of your world's solitude
of the endless present of your life;
then you left
opening my windows
clutching the clouds.

Below is the city and your ghosts;
the living slowly dying
from alcohol while sweet goodbyes
create a silence
clogged by lizards drowned in seaweed,
tearing sleeping fish
slowly breaking this wet earth

de presencias salinas
carcomiendo árboles y esperanzas,
dejando tan sólo, piedras, tumbas y enflaquecidos montes.

¡Oh esta sed del silencio!
Precisa de vivos, de manos cálidas
para alimentar un barro caído ha mucho tiempo.

Oh esta sed del silencio
que devora gritos para crear gritos
que precisa de llanto
para calmar el llanto.

Todos debemos, asidos del silencio,
abandonar nuestras palabras, nuestras armas,
para armar nuevos soldados
con un abecedario de existencias caídas.

Terrible destino:
morir para que la vida perdure,
qué glorioso destino,
mi muerte prolongará la vida
mis manos crearán otras manos
mis ojos otros ojos
mi voz que se apaga prolongará otras voces
y el montón de gritos apagados ascenderá hasta el cielo
y por él subirán los elegidos
y la tierra será digna morada de los hombres
la habrá forjado el llanto
de las gargantas despedazadas de los obreros
de las prostitutas,
destrozados por lo que creaban
con sus manos y sus sueños.

of saline life
rotting trees and hope,
left all alone: rocks, tombs, thinning mountains.

Oh, this thirst of silence
necessity of life, of warm hands
to nourish the mud fallen long ago.

Oh, this thirst of silence
that devours screams to create screams
that necessary cry
to calm the cry.

Gripped by this silence, we should all
abandon our words, our guns,
to arm new soldiers
with a language of lost existences.

Terrible destiny:
to die so life can endure,
what glorious destiny,
my death will prolong life
my hands will create other hands
my eyes other eyes
my voice fading away to prolong other voices
and the mass of fading shouts will ascend to the sky
and from them the chosen will rise
and the earth will be a worthy home for mankind
forged by the cry
from the shattered throats of the workers
of the women,
shattered for what they created
with their hands and their dreams.

SE VA AMONTONANDO EL SILENCIO

Se va amontonando el silencio
en la boca del pueblo
el cielo es una mordaza.
Las manos atadas
sangran
y se agrieta la vida
mientras la sangre va acumulando multitud de insectos.

La tierra esgrime su aliento
se niega a ser madre
los ríos se desbordan
y el hombre muere a cada minuto.
Los presidios se estremecen al contacto de un viejo amigo
que pace en su estrechez la amplia soledad de esta tierra.
El hombre espera cazando horas
hilvanando minutos
desatando palabras inhabitadas.

El pueblo languidece hambriento.
Pero nosotros
los comunistas
perseguidos
injuriados
alzamos nuestra voz enfrentando la muerte
por la vida
las cárceles
por la libertad.

Camaradas
un largo sendero dinamitado con odio
nos aguarda
nos esperan los fusiles y las bayonetas
para saciar en nuestra carne el infame apetito del Dollar

THE SILENCE IS BUILDING

The silence is building
in the village's mouth,
the sky a jaw.
Tied hands
are bleeding
life begins to crack
while blood summons a wave of insects.

The earth wields your breath
neglects its motherhood
rivers overflow
people die every minute.
Prisons shudder with the touch of an old friend
passing through its narrowness, the earth's wide solitude.
Man waits, hunting hours
stitching minutes
loosening uninhabited words.

The village languishes, haunted.
But we
the persecuted
injured
communists
raise our voices in the face of death
for life
for the imprisoned
for liberty.

Comrades
a long trail destroyed by hatred
awaits us
rifles and bayonets await us
to satiate the dollar's infinite appetite with our flesh.

Camaradas, en nosotros está la alborada
quieren matarla
matándonos
quieren guardarla en cajas de acero
asesinarla.

Camaradas, no os dejéis asesinar
alcémonos en nombre del pueblo con el pueblo.

Volved las espaldas a la noche
gritad: Patria te amamos
porque el pueblo te fue construyendo palmo a palmo
con su sangre se alimentó
Patria te arrancaremos de los barrotes.

Zurciremos los harapos que te cubren
para remendar nuestra bandera
y repitiendo siempre: Patria te amamos
escalaremos la sangre para darte vida.

Comrades, within us lives the dawn
they want to kill
by killing us
they want to trap it in a steel box
assassinate it.

Comrades, don't let them kill you
rise in the name of our people with our people.

Turn your backs to the night
shout: our homeland, we love you
we built you inch by inch
nourished by your blood
we'll tear you from the bars.

We'll take your rags
to mend our flag
repeating: our homeland, we love you
we'll scale the blood to give you life.

PERMANENCIA DEL LLANTO

I

¿En qué preciso momento se separó la vida de nosotros,
en qué lugar,
en qué recodo del camino?
¿En cuál de nuestras travesías se detuvo el amor
para decirnos adiós?
Nada ha sido tan duro como permanecer de rodillas.
Nada ha dolido tanto a nuestro corazón
como colgar de nuestros labios la palabra amargura.
¿Por qué anduvimos este trecho desprovisto de abrigo?
¿En cuál de nuestras manos se detuvo el viento
para romper nuestras venas
y saborear nuestra sangre?
Caminar... Hacia dónde?
¿Con qué motivo?
Andar con el corazón atado,
llagadas las espaldas donde la noche se acumula,
¿para qué?, ¿hacia dónde?,
¿Qué ha sido de nosotros?
Hemos recorrido largos caminos.
Hemos sembrado nuestra angustia
en el lugar más profundo de nuestro corazón.
¡Nos duele la misericordia de algunos hombres!
Conquistar nuevos continentes, ¿quién lo pretende?
Amar nuevos rostros, ¿quién lo desea?
Todo ha sido arrastrado por las rigolas.
No supimos dialogar con el viento y partir,
sentarnos sobre los árboles intuyendo próxima la partida.
Nos depositamos sobre nuestra sangre
sin acordamos de que en otros corazones el mismo líquido ardía
o se derramaba combatido y combatiendo.

PERMANENCE OF THE CRY

I

At what precise moment were our lives torn,
where,
at which bend in the road?
During which journey did love stop
to say goodbye?
Nothing has been as hard as living on our knees.
Nothing hurt our hearts more
than hanging bitter words from our lips.
Why did we wander this stretch of uncovered road?
In whose hand landed the wind
to tear our veins
and savor our blood?
Walk, to where?
Motivated by what?
Wandering with bound heart,
backs bruised by night,
where? What for?
What has happened to us?
We've come such a long way.
We've sown our anguish
in our heart's deepest chambers.
Wounded by the mercy of men.
Who's trying to conquer new continents?
Who desires to love new faces?
Everything dragged through the gutters.
We didn't know how to speak to the wind and leave,
sitting among the trees plotting our next departure.
We settle into our blood
forgetting the same fire burns in the hearts of others
spills from those who fought and those fighting.

¿Qué silencios nos quedan por recorrer?
¿Qué senderos aguardan nuestro paso?
Cualquier camino nos inspira la misma angustia,
el mismo temor por la vida.
Nos mutilamos al recogernos en nosotros,
nos hicimos menos humanidad.
Y ahora,
solos,
combatidos,
comprendemos que el hombre que somos
es porque otros han sido.

How many silences must we still traverse?
What roads await our steps?
All roads bring the same anguish,
the same fear for life.
We mutilated ourselves by lifting each other up,
we became less human.
And now,
alone,
fighting,
we understand that what we've become
is due to those who have been.

II

Ya no es necesario atar al hombre para matarlo.
Basta con apretar un botón
y se disuelve como montaña de sal bajo la lluvia.
Ni es necesario argüir que desprecia al amo.
Basta con proclamar -ceñuda la frente-
que comprometía la existencia de veinte siglos.
Veinte siglos,
dos mil años de combatida pureza,
dos mil años de sonrisas clandestinas,
dos mil años de hartura para los príncipes.
Ya no es necesario atar al hombre para matarlo.
La noche,
los rincones,
no,
nada de eso sirve ya.
Plazoletas y anchas calles se prestan bulliciosas.
No cuenta el asesinato con los pacientes,
no cuenta el príncipe con los sumisos.
Todos han olvidado que el hombre es aún capaz de cólera.
Las llamas se extinguen sin haber consumido el odio.
El día irredento ha postergado la resurrección del hombre.
Y los otros,
aquellos que presencian la matanza sentenciando:
"Locos, habéis tocado a la puerta de la muerte
y ella se quedó en vosotros!"
Esos
solo saben predecir la muerte,
no han aprendido a combatirla.
No han aprendido a cobijar la tierra en el corazón
ni a ganar la patria para el hombre.
Y el sumiso, ¿qué hace?
¿Dónde deposita su silencio?
¿En qué lugar del corazón teje la venganza?

II

You no longer have to tie a man down to kill him.
Stop pressing the button
and he will dissolve like a mountain of salt in rain.
You don't have to argue about who despises the master.
Enough proclamations— scowling—
compromising the existence of twenty centuries.
Twenty centuries,
two thousand years of fighting for innocence,
two thousand years of deception,
two thousand years of plenty for the princes.
You no longer have to tie a man down to kill him.
The night,
the corners,
no,
those are useless now.
Plazas and wide streets borrow their bustling.
Don't include the murdered with the patients,
don't include the princes with the peasants.
Everyone's forgotten the anger man is capable of.
The lamps extinguish without extinguishing hatred.
The unredeemed day has delayed man's resurrection.
And the others,
those that witness the murders:
"Lunatics, you've knocked on death's door
and now she lives with us!"
They
only know how to foretell death,
they haven't learned to fight her.
They haven't learned to hide the earth in their hearts
or win their homeland for themselves.
And what do the meek do?
Where do they deposit their silence?
In what depth of the heart do they weave their revenge?

Nadie lo sabe.
Todos le han olvidado.
Se ha dictaminado que su morada sea la sombra,
que el pan deshabitado sea su alimento,
que el pico le prepare el lecho
y la pala le cubra el corazón.
¿Qué es el hombre combatido?
Nadie lo recuerda.
Lo visten los trapos.
Lo arrojaron en la parte trasera de la casa
y allí
con los residuos
un guiñapo se amontona.
Las llamas se extinguen.
Se arrinconan los hombres en una sola sombra,
en un solo silencio,
en un solo vocablo,
en un llanto solo
y cuando todo sea uno,
uno el llanto y el vocablo uno
no habrá paz sobre la tierra.
¿No habrá paz?
Y aquellos que dictaminaron el destino del hombre,
los que jamás contaron con los sumisos,
amasarán con sangre su propia podredumbre.
¡No habrá paz!
¡Llanto para quebrar el llanto,
muerte para matar la muerte!

No one knows.
Everyone has forgotten.
It's been ruled that their dwelling will be the shadows,
that hollow bread will be their sustenance,
that birds will make their beds
and shovels will bury their hearts.
What is a fighting man?
No one remembers.
Dressed in rags.
Thrown to the back of the house
there
with the garbage
the wretched are piled.
The lamps are extinguished.
They've cornered themselves under a single shadow,
a single silence,
a single word,
a single cry
and when everything is one,
when the cry and the word are one
there will be no peace on earth.
There will be no peace?
Those who ruled on man's destiny,
those that would never sing with the meek,
will knead their own blood and rot.
There will be no peace.
Cry to end the cry,
die to kill death.

III

Las madres sintieron el temor de los hijos:
la diestra armada esgrimió su estandarte.
Unánime el corazón del mundo se levantaba.
Unánime, el llanto golpeaba las gargantas
y las palabras se quebraban como gaviotas perdidas.

Los hombres marchaban al encuentro con la vida;
La sangre del hermano pavimentaba el camino.
La vida quería entregarse,
repartirse por todas las urbes pobladas
y remozar aquellas que la muerte habitaba.
Había paredes para detenerla,
hachas para los brazos que osaban alcanzarla.

La diestra esgrimía su estandarte.
Los hijos del sol enterraban sus pies en la tierra:
eran troncos de una marcha que empezó con el hombre
y que aún permanece en su carne.

La sangre ha nacido para ser derramada,
la vida que se difunda.
El hijo,
para que sorprenda al crepúsculo del padre
y recoja lo que merece conservarse.

No ha sido posible contener el llanto.
Aún permanece la bestia en el trono.
Aún se quiebran las rodillas bajo el sol
y la prole no adivina que la morada es suya.

Callamos,
nos doblegamos
y un rumor de patria que se quiebra,
de espaldas combatidas,
de hembra que se corrompe
nos golpea.

III

The mothers felt their children's tremble:
the army wielding their banners in their right hands.
Unanimously, the world's heart rose.
Unanimously, the shout tore their throats
and their worlds shattered like lost seagulls.

The men marched on, searching for life;
the blood of their brothers paved the way.
Life wanted to surrender,
give itself to all the peopled cities
and resurrect those populated by death.
There were walls built for detainment
and axes for the arms that dared to reach.

Wielding banners in their right hands.
The sun's children bury their feet in the earth:
becoming trees from a march that began with man
and still stains their skin.

Blood was born to be spilled,
this diffusing life.
The child,
to shock the father's twilight
and collect what's worth collecting.

It's not possible to contain the cry.
Yet the beast won't be dethroned.
Yet knees still buckle beneath the sun
and the child doesn't know that this home is home.

Quietly,
we bow
and hear a whisper of our broken homeland,
of war-scarred backs,
of corrupt daughters
lashing us.

Todo ha sido falseado por los hombres de odio abundante.
Todo ha sido traducido en llanto.

¿Y las proles?
Crecen entre almendros y muros de cartón,
bajo techos que las estrellas perforan.
Crecen como las plantas y los arbustos
desterrados de la infancia,
desterrados de la urbe
que muchos hombres y muchas mujeres han levantado.

¿Qué ha sido del hombre?
¿Qué ha sido de la vida en esta tierra?
Nada ha permanecido tanto como el llanto.
¿Qué ha sido del hombre?
¿Qué ha sido de su morada y de su prole?

La tierra se ha hecho pródiga por su carne,
el suelo ha sido fecundo por su sangre,
los árboles han crecido desde su corazón derrumbado,
la han atado con sus venas al barro.

Unánime el corazón del mundo se levantaba,
tocaba las cimas.
La diestra armada esgrimía su estandarte,
esgrime,
golpeaba,
golpea,
la vida se precipitaba,
se precipita.

Everything is a lie from the many men of hatred.
Everything has been translated to a cry.

And the children?
They're raised among almond trees and cardboard walls,
under roofs perforated by stars.
They grow like plants and shrubs
exiled from childhood,
exiled from the city
raised by many men and women.

What has happened to mankind?
What has happened to life on this earth?
Nothing is as permanent as the cry.
What has happened to mankind?
What has happened to our home and our children?

The earth is lavished with our flesh,
the ground has become fertile with our blood,
trees grow from our caved-in hearts,
tied to the ground by our veins.

Together, the world's heart rose,
reaching the mountain peaks.
The army brandishing their banner,
wielding,
struck,
striking,
life is triggered,
life triggers.

V

Tengo miedo.
Han golpeado a tantos,
tanto y tanto caído,
tanto y tanto derrumbado.

Hemos padecido y habremos de padecer nuevamente,
todos lo sabemos
y sabemos también que la sonrisa no es nuestra,
que nunca ha estado en nuestros labios,
en nuestras manos.

¿Hay algún camino que conduzca a la alegría?
¿Hay alguna ruta desconocida?
No.
Todas han sido holladas por el hombre,
todas conducen a la alegría.
Aún no hemos llegado.
Hay muros, celdas y centinelas.

Que nadie piense que llega a la alegría con la alegría:
Cuesta mucho ser hombre.
Duele mucho querer la alegría.
Tengo miedo.
Tanto y tanto golpeado.
Tanto y tanto derrumbado.
Hace tiempo que dura esta marcha,
esta búsqueda incontrolable.

V

I'm scared.
They've hurt so many.
Countless fallen,
countless killed.

We have suffered and will suffer again,
we know this
and we know that this smile is not ours,
that it's never touched our lips
or been in our hands.

Is there a path toward happiness?
Is there some unknown route?
No.
Man has trampled everything,
everything that leads towards happiness.
We've never arrived.
There are only walls, cells, and sentries.

Let no one believe that joy brings joy:
it costs too much to be human.
It hurts too much to desire happiness.
I'm scared.
Countless hurt.
Countless killed.
This march goes on and on,
this uncontrollable searching.

VI

Que los hambrientos comprendan que la vida les pertenece.
Que el callado plañidor de las calles,
edifique con lo que nunca sus manos han tocado.
Que el viento socave al armazón del llanto.

Es preciso que el silencio deje de secundar nuestra voz.
Que las sombras depongan su hostil armadura ante la vida.
Precisamos de hombres tristes para hablar del hombre,
de mendigos trotamundos para combatir la bota.
Que los hombres de la tierra derriben los templos,
lancen corazones derribados a los dioses que predican
la muerte.
Pródiga la muerte que mata al que fecunda.
Pródigo el cañaveral que se alza devorándonos.
Pródiga la fiebre que nos consume,
a pesar de las raíces y de las hojas amargas.

Se han congregado los plañideros para abordar el día.
¿Cuál será el lugar que sus brazos ofrezcan,
cuál el camino que a recorrer invitan?
¿Qué preciado tesoro inventar con sus mentes afiebrada
para que yo,
sencillo mediador de palabras
adivine un silencio más largo que toda la sordera del mundo?

Tengo miedo.
Tanto y tanto golpeado
Tanto y tanto caído.

VI

That the hungry understand life belongs to them.
That the quiet mourners in the streets
raise what their hands never touch.
That the wind undermines the cry's scaffold.

Silence needs to stop seconding our voice.
That the shadows drop their hostile armor in the presence of life.
We need downed men to speak of man,
of wandering beggars fighting off boots.
That the people of this earth will tear down the temples,
launching their crushed hearts at the gods that preach
death.
Profuse is the death that kills what is fertile.
Profuse are the reedbeds that rise to devour us.
Profuse is the all-consuming fever,
weighed down by the roots and bitter leaves.

The mourners gather to approach the day.
Where are the open arms?
Which is the path that invites our passage?
What precious treasure can we invent with our fevered minds
so that I,
a simple mediator of words
can divine a silence larger than all the silences?

I'm scared.
Countless hurt.
Countless fallen.

Muchos creyeron en la posibilidad de la muerte.

Otros en la posibilidad del arribo.

Milenarias voces fatigadas levantaban un clamor.

Toda la genealogía de la tristeza combatía por la pureza.
Muchos antes de nosotros empujaron la barca,
otros después de nosotros continuarán empujándola.

No hemos sido los primeros,
no seremos los últimos ciertamente,
pero somos lo que del hombre no ha cesado de ser.
Los niños apretujaban su inabordable tristeza.
Sus rostros domeñaban los corceles,
mas la máquina arremetía.
¿Cómo reconquistar la vida para el hombre?
¿En qué lugar del corazón dar forma a la venganza?
¿En qué rincón deshabitado recomponer la alegría?

Toda la prole de los callejones,
toda la gente de la periferia,
toda la adolescencia de la tierra concurría al encuentro con la
vida,
y un olor a pureza machacada abundaba en el viento.
No ha habido tregua,
toda la prole acarició la sangre en los rostros amigos que
apetecían la vida.

Many believed in the possibility of death.

Others in the potential of arrival.

Thousands of tired voices raising turmoil.

All of sorrow's genealogy fights for innocence.
The multitude ahead of us pushes the boat,
and those behind us will push too.

We were not the first,
and we certainly won't be the last,
we are those who have not yet ceased to be.
The children clutch their unapproachable sorrow.
Their faces tame horses,
but the machines still attacked.
How to reconquer this life for mankind?
In which chamber of the heart does vengeance take shape?
In which empty corner can joy be rebuilt?

All the alley children,
all those living on the edge,
all the world's youth converge at this encounter with
life,
and the smell of crushed innocence fills the wind.
There's been no truce,
all the children caressing their friends' bloodied faces
who only want life.

Crecieron de pronto los niños de la patria.
Sus miradas se han hecho inexpresivas,
parecen continuamente azorados o ciegos.
Han comenzado a ver y a oír y a sentir,
ya saben que hay abundancia de dones,
que hay estrellas a la altura de sus cabecitas para guiar al
hombre,
que hay techos de dureza, manos, hombres y mujeres y aun
niños de dureza.

Han crecido ya los últimos testigos de estos días
la tierra tarda en prodigarse.
Las niñas también han crecido.
El sexo las acosa con fiebres,
sus vientres acumularon ventarrones.
Ahora hay collares en sus cuellos
y en sus ojos noche,
temblores en sus senos
y en sus ovarios muerte.
Volvió el hombre a su morada
con la antigua sensación de muerte en los labios.
Nada ha permanecido tanto como el llanto.
Hemos sido testigos del esfuerzo de unos brazos,
del hombre que mordiera el pavimento gritando la palabra
redentora.

The homeland's children grew quickly.
Their eyes expressionless,
They seem disturbed or blind.
They've begun to see and hear and feel,
they know there's an abundance of gifts,
that there are stars just above their heads to guide
mankind,
that there are tough roofs, hands, men and women and
hardened children.

The last witnesses of those days have grown
the land is slow to lavish.
The girls have grown too.
Harrassed by fevers of longing,
filled with hurricanes.
Now there are beads around their necks
and night in their eyes,
a trembling in their bodies
and dead ovaries.
Man returned home
with death's ancient touch on their lips.
Nothing is as permanent as the cry.
We've witnessed the striving of these arms,
of man who will bite down on the pavement
screaming the word of redemption.

VII

Aún transcurren los días sin que el hombre pueda contra el
llanto.
Se entrecruzan palabras batidas por el viento
y el amor padece el exilio del hombre.

Nada sabemos de aquellos que el odio abatiera.
Nada pudimos contra el poder del rencor.
Muchos de nuestros hijos fueron arrebatados,
mientras crepitaba en los crematorios la llama.
Todo parece inmóvil.
Siempre la misma estación de llanto y muerte.
Siempre la misma duración de agobios
¿Cómo despertar al hombre?
¿Cómo desatar el miedo que lo tiene amortajado?
Es preciso que rompamos el transcurso de estos días,
que combatamos el odio con las armas de la arcilla.

Los hijos más jóvenes se lanzaron en pos de la pureza.
Los padres temieron por el pan de cada día,
han aprendido a permanecer en la abstinencia.
Ya no comprenden que la primavera es posible.

Los hijos más jóvenes tomaron por asalto un día la alborada,
se proclamó el restablecimiento de la pureza y los ancianos
de esta tierra apenas comprendieron que la vida con sus
riesgos estaba con ellos.
Se han alzado brazos para detener la caída,
brazos modelados en los puertos a golpes de salitre,
brazos modelados en la fragua donde el acero
proclama su doblegada palabra.
Manos que de la tierra arrancaron la vida
repartiéndola entre las proles enfermas.

VII

Still the days go on with man unable to fight
the cry.
Broken words crisscrossed by the wind
and love suffers its exile from man.

We know nothing of those sunken by hatred.
We could do nothing against the power of their resentment.
Many of our children were torn away,
while flames crackled in the crematoriums.
Everything seems immovable.
Always the same seasons of cries and death.
Always the same duration of these burdens.
How do we awaken mankind?
How to cut off that shrouding fear?
We must break the course of passing days
and battle the earthen weapons of hatred.

The youngest children threw themselves toward innocence.
Parents feared for their daily bread,
they've learned to live restrained.
They no longer believe spring will come.

One day the young children took the dawn by force,
proclaimed the restoration of innocence and the old men
of this earth could barely comprehend that life with all
its risks was with them.
They put their arms out to break their fall,
arms molded in the ports by salted blows,
arms molded in the forge where steel
proclaims its doubled word.
Hands that pulled life from the earth
and gave it to the sick infants.

Ya no hay más que hombres combatidos que combaten.
Mujeres que han aprendido a proteger su sexo.
El odio multiplica sus centinelas para que el hombre
retorne a la sumisión.
Pero ya no es probable ese retorno.
Hemos aprendido que la primavera es posible.

There are no more soldiers still fighting.
Women have learned to protect themselves.
Hatred multiplies its sentries so that man
will return to submission.
But that return is no longer possible.
What we've learned: spring may still come.

VIII

Hemos ido acumulando corazones en nuestro corazón,
palabras en nuestra voz quebrantada por azadones.

Hemos dejado huellas por todos los caminos
y algunos de nosotros ya no estamos.
Hemos ido de manos con las sombras.
Nuestro andar es un grito estacionado.
Por cada paso, un día que transcurre.
Por cada palabra, mil palabras que vocifera la prole.
¿Qué será de nosotros después de esta larga travesía?
Poco importa si el mármol o la piedra eternizan
nuestro corazón de húmedo barro.
Nos basta con que nuestra voz perdure en la voz
del amigo, en la del compañero de rutas que nos tendió
la mano cuando se aproximaba la caída.

Hemos llenado muchos de los vacíos que nos legaran.
A otros toca llenar los que nosotros dejamos.
Apenas tuvimos tiempo para remendar la herencia.
¿A qué corazón irá nuestro corazón a depositarse?
¿A qué silbido irá nuestro silbo a renovarse?
Nada sabemos,
cumplimos una jornada que empezó antes que nosotros
y que no concluirá con nosotros.

VIII

We've accumulated hearts in our hearts,
words in our voices cracked by a pickaxe.

We've left footprints on every path
and some of us have ceased to be.
We've gone hand in hand with the shadows.
Our wandering is an immovable shout.
For every step taken, a day passes.
For every word, the infant screams a thousand.
What will become of us after this long journey?
It doesn't matter if it's marble or rock that eternalizes
our wet clay hearts.
It's not enough that our voice remains in the voice
of a friend, in a companion who reached out
their hand when we approached the fall.

We've filled much of the voids left to us.
Others picked up what we left behind.
We barely had time to repair our inheritance.
In which heart did our hearts go to bury themselves?
To which whistle did our whistling go to renew itself?
No one knows,
we approach a day that began before us
and won't end with us.

IX

El hombre camina amasando con caliche la palabra redentora.
Doblega la vida con sus manos rotas
y enarbola su pregón de vida mutilada.

Han colocado su cabeza en canas
La ofrecen en pública subasta.
Han colocado candelabros en su ruta
y cirios y mantos negros y argollas de acero.

No debe olvidar que sólo tiene un camino.
No debe dudar de que su vida es ajena,
que no le pertenece,
que nunca le ha pertenecido.

Y camina arrastrando su manto de pordiosero,
alimentado de fiebres y ancho cielo,
de palabras y callejuelas aullantes.
Y sin embargo, el hombre no ha nacido para morder el polvo
ni para silenciar la palabra.

No ha nacido para contemplar el llanto
sino para hacerlo grito,
arma que rompa los muros del dolor difundido.

Habrá que buscar al fabricante de la muestra.
Habrá que golpear aunque sea sin manos,
gritar aunque sea sin voz contra los que difunden el llanto
y guardan la sonrisa.
El hombre no ha podido reir,
le ha tocado tan solo morder el polvo.

IX

Man collects the redeeming word like pebbles.
Bending life with broken hands
and raising a cry of mutilated life.

They've placed their heads on canes
selling them at public auctions.
They've placed candelabras on the roadsides,
with candles and black cloaks and steel rings.

Don't forget you only have one path.
Don't doubt that your life is distanced,
that it has nothing to do with you,
that's it's never had anything to do with you.

Dragging its beggar's robes,
nourished by fevers and wide skies,
words and howling alleys.
Still, man wasn't born to eat dust
or silence the word.

He wasn't born to contemplate the cry
but rather to turn it into a shout,
a weapon to break down walls of diffused pain.

We have to search for the fabric of death.
We have to strike without hands,
shout without a voice against those who diffuse the cry
and hide their smiles.
Man has been unable to laugh
left with the lonely lot of eating dust.

Mirad el corazón del hombre,
es un puñado de sangre bajo el cielo.
Mirad el corazón del hombre:
es una estrella postrada sobre su propia sombra.

Miradlo,
es una lágrima que corre sobre raíles enmohecidos.
Mirad el corazón del hombre,
es nudo de ira atrapado por la sangre.
Hombre, he aquí tu rostro;
Mujer, he aquí tu carne;
Joven corajudo, he aquí tu tumba recién cavada.
Oh, pobre muchacho, no dejaste tu semen frutecido en la tierra:
No pudiste sembrarte en la mujer que amabas.
¡No te dieron tiempo!
Pero no importa.
Yo me declaro tu hijo
y en tu nombre elevaré mi voz
porque en mi nombre sellaron tus labios.

See the human heart,
a fistful of blood under sky.
See the human heart:
a star laid over its own shadow.

See it,
a tear running down a moldy rail.
See the heart of man,
knotted, trapped in blood.
Man, your face is here;
woman, your body is here;
brave youth, your grave is newly dug.
Oh, poor boy, no chance to inseminate the earth:
no chance to love the woman you love.
You were given no chance.
But that doesn't matter.
I declare myself your son
and in your name I raise my voice,
in my name your lips were sealed.

X

A Rafael Campusano

Dulce la tierra que protege
la disgregada muchedumbre de células que tú animaste
y por el sendero marcado por los glóbulos
edifica pesados silencios
para los que aún permanecen.

Ahora no sé dónde encontrarte,
si en la luminosa trayectoria de las lunas dormidas
o en la impenetrable dureza de las sombras,
Quizás
hayas dejado recuerdo hecho piedra
donde puedan mis manos de tiempo en tiempo
acariciarte el rostro anochecido.

¿Por qué hubo llanto en tu vida?
Tus ojos y tu carne chorreaban lagrimones
como para ahogar muchedumbres,
como para lavar al mundo.
Cada lágrima tuya abría nichos en la tierra,
soles terrenales fragmentaba,
voces de recobrada dulzura.
¿Escuchas, amigo, lo que ahora mi corazón proclama,
el silencio que recopila recuerdos
y anuda en la garganta miles de voces?
¿Escuchas este clamor, hombre de testa sombría
donde crecen flores y plantas oscuras,
donde la savia reconstruye la trayectoria de la sangre?
Escuchas, amigo mío,
de esta permanencia de luces y sombras,
de combates que nunca se deciden,

X

for Rafael Campusano

Sweet is the land that protects
the disintegrated crowd of cells you animated
and the path marked by drops of blood
large silences erected
for those that still remain.

Now I don't know where to find you,
in the luminous trajectory of sleeping moons
or in the impenetrable hardness of shadows,
maybe
you've left a keepsake made of rock
where, from time to time, my hands
can caress your face of dusk.

Why was this crying in your life?
Your eyes and skin poured tears
to drown the masses,
to wash the world.
Each of your tears opens a slit in the earth,
fragmented suns,
voices of regained sweetness.
Can you hear, my friend, what my heart is saying now,
this silence collecting memories
knotting thousands of voices in my throat?
Can you hear this clamoring, shadowed mind
where dark flowers grow,
where sap reconstructs blood?
Can you hear, my friend,
this permanence of light and shadow,
these endless battles,

de ideas y retornos,
de este lento transcurso de sollozos
el recobrado clamor de los hombres todos
reclamados para discutir tu palabra,
levantar osamentas
y cavar fosas para muertos grandes?

Escucha.
Debes escuchar,
es tuyo este silencio que subleva,
ruido que adormece desde nuestras manos naciendo.
Tuyos estos corazones que alberga la herencia,
tuya esta permanencia del coraje,
tuyos
todos estos brazos y piernas,
y bocas y ojos que quieren multiplicarte,
que quieren reconstruirte,
recobrarte
con lágrimas
y palabras y quejidos.
¿Escuchas?
Debes escuchar desde tu momento de enmudecido pregonero,
inalterable presencia de las sombras.

Escucha,
lo que de ti guardaron los ecos,
lo que de nosotros no pudiste llevarte.
No volverás,
no, no volverás!
No retorna el viento con las palabras pronunciadas,
estás mudado, mudado de belleza,
mudado de tristeza,
en definitiva permanencia de siglos establecido.

these ideas and returns,
this slow sobbing
this recovered clamor of all those
reclaimed to discuss your word,
raising bones
and digging large graves for the dead?

Listen.
You should listen,
this rebellious silence is yours,
noise that numbs from our born hands.
Yours are the hearts that house the inheritance,
yours is this permanence of courage,
yours
all these arms and legs,
and mouths and eyes that desire to multiply,
that want to rebuild,
recover
with tears
and words and complaints.
Are you listening?
You should listen from your time of muted tears,
inalterable presence of shadows.

Listen,
to what the echoes hide from you,
to what you couldn't lift from us.
You won't return,
no, you won't return.
The wind won't return speaking those words,
you're moved, moved by beauty,
moved by sadness,
in defined permanence of set centuries.

¿Quién predijo que los hijos de la tierra
rencor anidarían en el corazón?
¿Quién supuso la existencia del moho
cuando fuimos congregados para hablar del amor?
¿Quién predijo, pero quién,
el nacimiento de estos hombres a la pura permanencia,
en pleno día,
ante todos nosotros que ahora sollozamos,
ante todos nosotros que ahora nos interrogamos?
¿Escuchas?
Debes escuchar, amigo, hermano,
camarada de la dura jornada,
es tuyo este clamor de hombres mudos gesticulando,
de mujeres vendadas difundiendo ternuras,
de lámparas sin gas parcelando la luz.
¿Quién predijo, pero quién,
esta mudanza terrible del hombre en criatura del odio?

Who predicted that the earth's children
would nest resentment in their hearts?
Who knew this mold existed
when we gathered to speak of love?
Who, who predicted
those born into pure permanence,
in the light of day,
before all of us sobbing,
before all of us questioning ourselves?
Are you listening?
You should listen friend, brother,
comrade of difficult days,
yours is the clamor of mute gesturing men,
bandaged women diffusing tenderness,
gasless lamps parceling light.
Who, who predicted
this terrible transformation of man into a creature of hatred?

XI

Hablo del abatimiento que se cumple en nosotros,
de lo que no ha sido por culpa de nuestro silencio,
de lo que ha muerto porque nuestro corazón no quiso
emprender la marcha.

Hablo ahora para todos
del agobio que se cumple en nosotros,
del abatimiento de la luz en la morada del hombre.
Nos encerramos en nuestra anatomía,
tapamos nuestros poros
para que ni el aire saboreara el poco de luz heredado.
Hemos pagado caro nuestro miedo de morir.
Hemos pagado caro nuestro derecho de estar solos,
a no sentir y a no ver,
a no escuchar siquiera.

Hoy
cuando en nosotros se cumple la quebradura del canto
aprendemos lo que cuesta abandonar al hombre.
No supimos ser comensales del fuego
y hemos sido comensales del llanto.
Hemos pagado caro nuestro orgullo.
Ya no son más que sombras y polvo
los que establecieron la posibilidad del canto.
Hemos pagado caro nuestro miedo de morir.
Ganamos una muerte más dura que la tumba.

XI

I speak of dejection actualized in us,
of what hasn't been because of our silence,
of what has died because our hearts
didn't want to ignite the march.

I speak now for everyone
of the burden actualized in us,
of the dejected light in our homes.
We lock ourselves into our anatomy,
we clam up
so even the air won't know how little light we inherit.
We've paid dearly for our fear of death.
We've paid dearly for our right to be alone,
and not feel or see,
not even listen.

Today
when within us the ruptured song is fulfilled
we'll learn the cost of abandoning our fellow man.
We didn't know how to eat fire
and instead ate the cry.
We've paid dearly for our pride.
Now there's nothing but dust and shadows
left of those who created the possibility of the song.
We've paid dearly for our fear of death.
We've earned a harder death than the grave.

XII

Crecemos abatiendo corazones
y a medida que nos alejamos de los lugares comunes,
crece la herida, que heredamos de nuestro padre
y de aquellos que no fueron nuestro padre.
Cierra los párpados el niño que duerme en nosotros
y comenzamos a hilvanar caminos.
Nuestra herencia se compone de algunas palabras,
de algún abuelo corajudo
o de algún hombre que estableció sobre esta tierra
su derecho a la vida.

Nada poseemos
y sin embargo podemos modelar
o levantar pirámides para cobijar el pasado
quebrar el llanto que se cumple en nosotros.

El hombre vino desposeído de armaduras.
Vino con chillidos que se hicieron palabras.
Vino confiando y comenzó sonriendo la jornada.

No tardó mucho el llanto. No se hizo esperar la bestia.

Ahora debemos levantar la lumbre con nuestras manos hechas
para quemarse,
derrumbar las alambradas hechas para dividirnos
y devolver al niño su palabra de niño,
su juguete de niño:
nada de acorazados infantiles
ni de espadas reducidas.

Flores para su frente y colores para burlar el sol
y cantos y sonrisas para que las difundan.
Para que disminuya la fatiga del padre,
para que contenga la lágrima de la madre que hila.
Nada poseemos y sin embargo podemos modelar.

XII

We grow demolished hearts
to distance ourselves from common places,
wounds grow that we inherit from our fathers
and those who weren't our fathers.
The child sleeping within us closes their eyes
begins to sew the roads.
Our inheritance is made up of words,
from some courageous grandfather
or some man who claimed on this land
the right to live.

We own nothing
but still we can build
pyramids to shelter the past
break the cry that breeds in us.

Man arrived dispossessed of his armor.
He arrived with a shrieking that became words.
He arrived with trust and smiled at the day.

The cry didn't last. The beast did not wait.

Now we should raise the fire with our hands made
for burning,
tear down the barbed wires meant to divide us,
return the child's words to the child,
the child's toy to the child:
no more battleships manned by children
or worn-down swords.

Flowers for your head vibrant enough to laugh at the sun
and songs and smiles to spread around.
To relieve the fatigue of our fathers,
to hold the row of tears in our mothers.
We own nothing and yet we can build.

XIII

Hemos derramado la simiente a la puerta del crematorio.
El sol se ha depositado en los pinos empujando al viento.
El viento trae el olor a humus de la entraña del continente.
Olor que se ha ido alimentando de nuestra carne por siglos.
Hay humedad en el viento,
humedad de ríos y riachuelos acurrucándose en la piedra.
Humedad de cielo y tierra apareándose,
de planta recién brotada,
humedad de tubérculo naciente.
El sol y la tierra apareándose para que la vida permanezca.
Sol y tierra para que el hombre acumule bondades.
¡Cómo ha cambiado el destino de esta tierra!
Sol y tierra:
sol para alumbrar muertos que navegan por rigolas.
Tierra para acogernos sin protesta.
¿Y el viento?
Dispersando polvo indiscriminadamente.
¡Cuidado!
Hay polvo de hombre en el polvo del mundo.
¿Quién ha cambiado el rumbo del viento?
¿Quién dispuso cerrojo para los graneros?
¿Quién desvió la daga hacia el corazón del hombre?

Hay hombres acaparando el día.
Hay hombres bestias doblegando la ternura,
cabalgaduras de aluminio llevando la muerte,
trompetas de oro anunciando que la vida concluye.
Han sido sometidos los portadores de palabra,
aquellos que pensaron que bastaba decir la palabra
para que todos la oyeran y la amaran.

XIII

We've planted our seed at the crematorium's door.
The sun deposits itself in pines that push the wind.
The wind brings the smell of smoke from the continent's entrails.
A stench that has fed on our flesh for centuries.
There's a humidity in the air,
a humidity of rivers and creeks smothering rocks.
A humidity of sky mating with the earth,
of newly sprouting plants,
a humidity birthing roots.
The sun and earth mate so that life can go on.
Sun and earth so that people can gather kindness.
How the earth's destiny has altered!
Sun and earth:
sun to give light to the dead navigating the gutters.
Earth to welcome us without complaint.
And the wind?
Indiscriminately blowing dust.
Careful!
There is human dust in the dust of the world.
Who has altered the wind's route?
Who ordered the barns bolted shut?
Who aimed the dagger at the hearts of man?

There are men hoarding daylight.
There are beastly men beating down tenderness,
riding the aluminum that carries the dead,
golden trumpets announcing the end of life.
The word bearers have been subdued,
those who thought speaking the word was enough
so everyone would hear and love.

XIV

Hubo una ciudad bajo una lluvia de recuerdos.
Hay una ciudad bajo una lluvia de sangre.
La divide el agua llenándola de aromas acuosos,
lavando muros y hombres.
Hay una ciudad bajo una lluvia de sangre,
abandonando la madera y las lianas,
alcanzando el ladrillo y el cemento.
Prolongadas raíces de hierro escudriñan la tierra
y soportan elevadas palabras de sílice y cal.
Aquí hace tiempo que la vida viene mutilándose
Se escuda en las cunas.
Padece en los hospitales.
Y se va repitiendo. Se marcha. Retorna. Avanza.
Prostitutas hermosas como caracoles abundan en sus calles.
Vagos que acechan el de la pureza.
En los palacios, en las asambleas,
corazones muertos proclaman la necesidad del silencio.
Nada habremos de aprender de los lectores que enmudecen.
Nada arrancaremos a los hombres de frac que no sean rosas
muertas.
¿Cómo levantar los muertos en una insurrección de sombras
en contra de la muerte?
¿Cómo edificar la vida en estas latitudes del odio?
Se dilata la urbe y la alegría se contrae.
La ciudad está desnuda,
desnuda de palabras, desnuda de hombres con vigor en las venas.
Abundan cazadoras nocturnas, vagos sin ley ni palabra.
¡Ah! Y niños que deambulan asombrados,
cabecitas despeinadas aprendiendo la noche,
preguntando a los ancianos el nombre de las constelaciones.
Miradas dulces como de estanque,
sin larvas ni musgo, sin naufragios.

XIV

There was a city under a rain of memories.
There is a city under a rain of blood.
The aroma-filled water was divided,
washing the walls and people.
There is a city under a rain of blood,
abandoned to woods and vines,
which reach for the bricks and cement.
Long iron roots tear through the earth
raising words of silica and lime.
It's been a long time since mutilated life arrived,
hiding in a crib.
Suffering in hospitals.
And it repeats. It goes on. It returns. It advances.
Gorgeous sex workers gathered in the streets like snails.
Bums that stalk the streets of innocence.
In the palaces, in the assemblies,
dead hearts proclaim the need for silence.
Nothing to learn from a mute audience.
Nothing ripped from men in suits that's not
a dead rose.
How to raise the dead in an insurrection of shadows
to fight against death?
How to raise life in these latitudes of hatred?
The city expands and joy contracts.
The naked city,
stripped of words, stripped of men with vigor in their veins.
Nocturnal hunters abound, lawless, wordless bums.
Ah! And children that wander in astonishment,
their small disheveled heads lighting up the night,
asking their elders the names of the stars.
The sweet look of a lake,
without larvas or moss or shipwrecks.

Todo esto por las calles.
La vida, el cieno, la pureza.
Ciudad edificada al borde de las aguas,
por hombres de duros bronces y brillantes arcabuces.
No hay monumentos mas que para el conquistador
o el cruel guerrero que pariera esta tierra en su transcurso.
Bronces para la espada y las armas todas,
nada para el rostro de algún niño o de algún jovenzuelo que
creció asustado
o de alguna muchacha que murió pariendo.
Toda una ciudad para la muerte.
Patios sin parcela para el juego.
Parque con estrechos cementerios y árboles descuidados
para amantes pordioseros o escapados dementes.
Urbe dividida por las aguas. Muros que golpean.
Hombres dibujando caminos,
mujeres cargadas de semen maldito.
Oh ciudad
toda una necrópolis para el hombre!

All this in the streets.
Life, mud, innocence.
City built on the water's border,
by men with hard bronze and brilliant rifles.
There are only monuments to the conquistadors
or the cruel warrior birthed in the course of this land.
Bronze for every sword and weapon,
nothing for the face of a child
who grew up in fear
or girls dying in labor.
Everything a city of death.
Backyards with no room to play.
Parks filled with graves and dead trees
for deprived lovers or escaped lunatics.
City divided by water. Painful walls.
Men drawing paths,
women carrying evil seeds.
Oh city
all a necropolis for man.

XV

Calles.
Pasos que se combaten.
Puertas y ventanas entornadas.
Viento que a hurtadillas sustrae las palabras.
Es invierno.
Mugre en los cerrojos de la luz.
Temblor de labios.
Cantos que se derrumban.
Quebradura de alas.
Calles,
edificios altos y opacos,
Plazoletas, niños que juegan en la tarde,
balones que se elevan alzando la pureza de la tierra.
Húmedos resplandores en el crepúsculo.
Temblores nacientes
en la noche de entumecida sombra.
Calles,
hombres y mujeres apretujándose.
Temor que cunde en los huesos.
Temor en los barrios altos de casas pequeñas y tristes.
Temor en la carne estrujada desprovista de abrigo
Calles,
edificios opacos,
días largos como estremecimientos,
palabras agarrotadas,
soledad sola.
Llanto.
Calles,
Altos barrios con sus hombres y mujeres de miedo.
con sus niños y sus niñas de miedo,
con sus casas de pesado cielo azul,
con su penumbra de estrellas lejanas.
Calles.
Abandonada soledad.
Llanto.

XV

Streets,
footfalls of war.
Doors and windows boarded up.
Wind that sneakily steals our words.
It's winter.
Dirt in locks of light.
Trembling lips.
Collapsing songs.
Breaking wings.
Streets,
tall opaque buildings,
plazas, children playing in the evening,
balls flying through the air, lifting the pure earth.
Humidity radiating in twilight.
New tremblings
in this night of numb shadows.
Streets,
men and women embracing.
Fear that spreads to the bone.
Fear in the high villages of small sad houses.
Fear in the crushed, unclothed body.
Streets,
opaque buildings,
long shivering days,
cluttered words,
lonely solitude.
Crying.
Streets,
high villages with fearful men and women,
with their fearful boys and girls,
with homes of heavy blue sky,
with the gloom of far-off stars.
Streets,
abandoned to solitude.
Crying.

XVI

Dura brisa,
rumiante nave de transparentes remos,
hiende el espacio con tu quilla de alientos
y muéstrame el corazón vagabundo.

Dura brisa,
peregrina nave,
muéstrame el polvo de otros continentes,
las hojas de otros árboles.
Acumula en mí los olores de otra selva,
de otros bosques,
quiero penetrar en todo lo que nunca mis ojos han tocado,
en todo lo que me es lejano,
en toda lejanía.

Dura brisa,
frío temblor,
suave cristal resbalando por el espacio;
finísima lágrima de cielo rodando.
Peregrina,
muéstrame de otros lugares el llanto,
de otros lugares las lágrimas.
Quiero saber si pesan tanto como las nuestras,
si son tan puras de tan tristes.
Anda,
dame noticias del hombre de otros países,
de su cotidiano quehacer en su mundo.

XVI

Hard breeze,
ruminant ship with transparent oars,
cleave the space with your keel
and show me your vagabond heart.

Hard breeze,
migrant ship,
show me the earth of other continents,
the leaves of other trees.
Pour in me the aroma of other jungles,
other forests,
I want to enter everything my eyes never touched,
in everything distant to me,
in every distance.

Hard breeze,
cold shiver,
smooth crystal sliding through space;
fine tear of rolling sky.
Migrant,
show me the cry from elsewhere,
from other places and other tears.
I want to see if they're as heavy as ours,
if they're as pure and sad.
Go on,
tell me the news of people in other countries,
of the daily lives in their world.

Dura brisa,
cristal de frío en diciembre,
acumulado aliento,
tráeme el sabor de otros labios,
el vaho amargo de otros continentes,
el grito de los hombres,
arrastra hasta mí lo que de combatida pureza permanezca
abandonado.

Dura brisa,
rumiante nave de transparentes remos
peregrina,
con todas tus regiones,
con todas sus selvas y bosques poblados de sierpes y flores,
de frutos y aves, con todos tus peces y tus islas
acumúlate en mi corazón,
cobija en él tu memoria.

Hard breeze,
December's cold crystal,
accumulating breath,
bring me the touch of other lips,
the bitter mist of other continents,
the human shout,
drag what purity and permanence
abandoned together.

Hard breeze,
ruminant ship with transparent oars,
migrant,
with all your regions,
with all your jungles and forests covered in serpents and flowers,
with fruits and birds, with all your fish and islands
make room for yourself in my heart,
blanket it in your memory.

XVII

Hombres.
vuestras manos tiznadas de negro.
carbón humanizado.
golpean la dureza del tiempo transcurrido.
Hombres.
hay rumor de quebradura en los huesos.
polvo naciendo en nuestro cuerpo.
de nuestro cuerpo
como de sumergida sal.
Hombres.
dejad vuestro nombres en el gran libro del llanto.
derribad la pirámide levantada con sangre.
negad con las manos tiznadas.
con la palabra combatida
antes de que el polvo se desprenda del corazón.
El viento apaga las ascuas de nuestro cuerpo.
revienta nuestros labios
arranca nuestro peto,
hebra tras hebra,
y las va juntando
y las va atando
hasta hilvanar una larga palabra que entumece los oidos.
Aún hay tiempo de decir la palabra.
Hombre, apresúrate,
asume la herencia sin temor,
levántate,
no te derrumbes,
aún hay tiempo,
di la palabra,
hazte ciudadano del mundo,
asume su dolor,
su llanto,

XVII

Men,
our blackened hands,
humanized carbon,
hammering against the hardened passage of time.
Men,
there are rumors of broken bones,
dust born in our bodies,
from our bodies
like submerged salt.
Men,
we'll leave our names in the great book of the cry,
raze the pyramids raised by blood,
destroy them with our blackened hands,
with combative words
before the dust is unpinned from our hearts.
The wind blows out the embers of our bodies,
cracking our lips
pulling our hair
strand by strand
collecting
and tying it
until a word large enough to numb our ears emerges.
There's still time to say the word.
Men, hurry,
claim your inheritance without fear,
rise,
do not collapse,
there's still time,
say the word,
become a citizen of the world,
claim your pain,
your cry,

sé sufragante de su vida,
de su protesta levanta el clamor,
abriga su minuto.
sé complice de su sonrisa.
abraza su locura,
sé sufragante de su estatura.
Hombre.
no te derrumbes.
Es preciso estar con los demás.
Duele el aunarse
golpea el amar.
Se cómplice del amor.
Es el único medio de salvar la vida.

your life's suffering,
your protests will raise the riots,
harboring this moment.
Complicit with your smiles,
embrace your madness,
your heightened suffering.
Men,
do not collapse.
It's crucial to stand united,
uniting hurts,
love is painful,
but be love's accomplice
it's the only way to save your lives.

XVIII

Tapamos nuestros oídos a todo ruido.
Permanecimos quietos
                        cuando el hombre reclamaba nuestra mano,
nuestro brazo.
No supimos arriesgar el caserón,
ni siquiera preguntamos por los que de pronto dejaron de verse.

Somos la mugre que alardea,
crepúsculo que tarda en naufragar.
Han crecido las lianas en los patios.
El agua se ha poblado de larvas
y de huevecillos temblorosos,
el aire de quejidos.
El campo y la ciudad han parcelado el silencio
y cada ciudadano hace uso de su parcela.
No hay palabra,
no hay hombres,
solo puertas entornadas.
Tapamos nuestros oidos,
nuestros ojos,
podremos decir: nada vimos, nada escuchamos
y regalar lágrimas a las viudas
y entonar cánticos a la gloria
cuando el hombre pregunte por los que no estuvieron
        en el momento del dolor.

Por los que nada vieron ni oyeron.
Quién ha dicho que puede cruzar el pantano sin enlodarse,
que se puede cambiar bajo la lluvia sin mojarse?
Quién ha dicho que nada se compromete con no ver y no escuchar?
Que nadie alegue ignorancia.
El hombre estuvo a nuestro lado con su grito a cuestas.
Los que no vieron que padezcan por no haber visto.
Los que no escuharon que padezcan por no haber escuchado
Los que no han padecido que padezcan por no haber padecido.
Adviene el tiempo de la siembra.
Es preciso limpiar la tierra de cizaña.

XVIII

We shut our ears to the noise.
We stay quiet
                when the man reclaims our hand,
our arm.
We didn't know how to risk the barracks,
we didn't even ask about those who disappeared.

We are the flaunting dirt,
the twilight that's slow to sink.
Vines overgrow the backyards.
The water is dusted with larva
and from these trembling eggs
comes the whining air.
The town and the city have parceled their silence
and every citizen makes use of their parcel.
There are no words,
there are no men,
only doors left ajar.
We shut our ears,
our eyes,
we can say: we saw nothing, we heard nothing
and gift tears to the windows
and sing hymns of glory
when they ask about those that weren't
                there in that painful moment.

For those who heard and saw nothing:
who said you can stay clean while crossing the swamp,
that you can change clothes in the rain and stay dry?
Who said nothing is compromised by not seeing or hearing?
May no one claim ignorance.
Man was by our side with his screams.
May those who say nothing suffer for not seeing.
May those who heard nothing suffer for not listening.
May those who haven't suffered suffer for their avoidance.
Now arrives the time of sowing.
It's crucial to rid the earth of weeds.

IXX

Salvo la palabra del hombre.
Todo ha concluido en estas regiones.
Sobre la tierra los árboles y los niños.
Bajo tierra...los hombres.
Todo ha transcurrido como si nada temiera la muerte.
Fue tan abundante la cosecha del odio.
tan numerosa la prole catafalcos.
Todos tocó sangre,
a todos tocó silencio.
Volvió la vida a la tierra.
Volvió la palabra al silencio.
Volvió la luz a la tiniebla.
Qué labor emprender ahora que el hombre concluye esta jornada?
Los muertos no llaman a los vivos.
Han dejado de escudriñar.
Nosotros les prestamos pensamientos y palabras.
Los muertos no apetecen.
No piden. Son los vivos quienes precisan
de nuestra palabra.
La vida se derrumba,
algo queda,
hay una herencia que defender.
Nombres que prolongar.
Ay de nosotros sino recogemos la simiente abatida,
si no modelamos con polvo de nombre
el corazón que la tierra reclama.
Hombres,
avivad el fuego.
Mujer, ata a tus ovarios semen yal corajudo
que la vida exige ser vida,
que el amor proclama la necesidad de ir más allá de nuestras vidas.

IXX

I save the word of man.
Everything comes to an end here.
Atop the dirt are trees and children.
Below the dirt— men.
Everything happened as though no one feared death.
A bountiful harvest of hatred,
the bier's offspring inumerable.
All touch blood,
silence touches all.
Life returned to earth.
The word returned to silence.
Light returned to void.
What work can be started now that the sun is setting?
The dead do not call to the living.
They no longer look closely.
We lend them thoughts and prayers.
The dead crave nothing.
Ask for nothing. It's the living that need
our words.
Life is overthrown,
but something remains,
there's an inheritance to defend.
Names to continue.
Woe is us if we don't recover that dejected seed,
if we don't mold from the dust of our names
that heart that the earth is reclaiming.
Men,
light the fires.
Women, reclaim your bodies; and to the brave
life demands to be lived,
love demands we outlive our own lives.

MARCHO FATIGADO

Marcho fatigado,
busco donde asirme,
toco la piedra y me hiere,
miro la luz y me ciega,
abrazo la sombra
y siento que me diluyo,
que comienza el minuto terrible de hacerme polvo.

FATIGUED MARCH

Fatigued march,
I look for something to cling to,
I touch the rock and am wounded,
I see the light and am blinded,
I embrace the shadows
and feel that it dilutes me,
that the terrible moment of becoming dust has arrived.

Acknowledgments

Grateful acknowledgment is made to the following literary magazines and entities where some of these poems first appeared, sometimes in earlier forms:

The Acentos Review: "My Homeland Arose"
Asymptote: "Man Awakens," "We Take Refuge"
The Cortland Review: "From the Mountains"
Four Way Review: "Song for America"
Islandia: "Fatigued March"
Jewish Currents: "You Arrived"
Lost & Found: Light Relief: "For an Assassinated Black Leader," "Permanence of the Cry: XVII, XVIII, IXX"
Moko: Caribbean Arts and Letters: "Permanence of the Cry: I, II, & III"
Sinking City: "I'm Trying to Tell You About My Homeland," "The Rain"
Solstice: "Homeland," "The Dead"

Thank You

Thank you to Roberto Carlos and Get Fresh Books for believing in the work. Thank you to the Manship Summer Research Fellowship at LSU, which allowed me to complete this book. Thank you to my teachers at Queens College Roger Sedarat and Annmarie Drury for their feedback on this project, and especially to my thesis advisor Ammiel Alcalay for seeing the importance of this work and championing it at every opportunity. Thank you to everyone at the CUNY Lost & Found Project. Thank you to the family of Jacques Viau Renaud, Michelle Viau and Clemente Viau, for allowing me to bring this poetry to a wider audience. And of course, thank you to my dad, Francisco Henriquez, for introducing me to Jacques Viau Renaud.

Ariel Francisco is the author of *All the Places We Love Have Been Left in Ruins* (Burrow Press, 2024), *Under Capitalism If Your Head Aches They Just Yank Off Your Head* (Flowersong Press, 2022), and *A Sinking Ship is Still a Ship* (Burrow Press, 2020), and the translator of Haitian-Dominican poet Jacques Viau Renaud's *Poet of One Island* (Get Fresh Books, 2024) and Guatemalan poet Hael Lopez's *Routines/Goodbyes* (Spuyten Duyvil, 2022). A poet and translator born in the Bronx to Dominican and Guatemalan parents and raised in Miami, his work has been published in *The New Yorker, American Poetry Review, Academy of American Poets, POETRY Magazine, The New York City Ballet, Latino Book Review,* and elsewhere. He is Assistant Professor of Poetry and Hispanic Studies at Louisiana State University.

www.ingramcontent.com/pod-product-compliance
Lightning Source LLC
Chambersburg PA
CBHW041831110726
48006CB00020B/2589